God's Word
for the
Unmarried Believer™

D1092707

God's Word
for the
Unmarried Believer™

West Bloomfield, Michigan

WARNER BOOKS

An AOL Time Warner Company

Copyright © 2003 by Warner Books, Inc.,
with Walk Worthy Press
All rights reserved.

Published by Warner Books, Inc.,
with Walk Worthy Press™
*Real Believers, Real Life,
Real Answers in the Living God* ™

Walk Worthy Press, 33290 West Fourteen Mile Road,
482, West Bloomfield, MI 48322

Warner Books, Inc., 1271 Avenue of the Americas,
New York, NY 10020

Visit our Web sites at www.walkworthypress.net and
www.twbookmark.com

An AOL Time Warner Company

Printed in the United States of America
First Printing: October 2003
10 9 8 7 6 5 4 3 2 1

Library of Congress Cataloging-in-Publication Data
God's Word for the unmarried believer /
the editors of Walk Worthy Press.
p. cm.
Originally published: West Bloomfield, MI :
Walk Worthy Press, 2001.
ISBN 0-446-69236-0
1. Single people—Religious Life. 2. Christian life—
Biblical teaching. I. Walk Worthy Press.
BV4596.S5G63 2003
242'.64—dc21   2003045064

Book design and text composition by Cassandra Pappas
Cover illustration by Elizabeth Rosen

To Evangelist Kathryn Stramler,
who not only introduced me and
countless others to the biblical principles
of living godly and unmarried,
but who also lives a life that continues
to set the example.

And to Minister Lois Vaughn,
who truly blessed me and confirmed
the vision for this work with her words
of encouragement.

Thanks you.

DLS

Acknowledgments

THERE WERE MANY PEOPLE responsible for putting this little but powerful book together.

Although the names are changed, the stories are real, and I want to thank those who shared their hearts with us.

In addition:

Thank you, Gloria Pruett, for your hard work, enthusiasm, and love for the Word of God.

Special appreciation to Carol Mackey, for caring enough to make those lunches and dinners more than "just business."

Thank you, friends Bean, Boogaloo Ann, Pit Bull Cynthia, and Prayer Warrior Janie, for constantly pushing (in a good way), encouraging (sometimes in a loud way), and loving (always in a godly way)!

This one is for all of you.

Contents

Introduction

> For I would that all men were even as I myself. But every man hath his proper gift of God, one after this manner, and another after that. I say therefore to the unmarried and widows, it is good for them if they abide even as I. But if they cannot contain, let them marry: for it is better to marry than to burn.
>
> I CORINTHIANS 7:7-9

THE TWO MOST "single" people in the Bible were Jesus and the Apostle Paul, and what Paul told the Corinthians is very different from what most of us have grown up thinking. Many of us have somehow gotten it into our heads that marriage and finding husbands or wives is something that we *must* do. Many unmarried believe that if that does not happen, we are personal failures and incomplete in Christ.

Often, in "singles" groups, the main focus is on people getting together or being matched up, and many of the teachings and activities revolve around dating. The thing about it is this: Too many unmarried Christians are unhappy and confused because they do not feel that they are capable of living in the fullness of God without a mate.

Many do not understand that it is God's will for them to be happy with or without a mate. We have the assurance in His Word that we can be unmarried and happy in Him doing what He has called us to do.

There are a slew of books that advise married believers on how to operate in Godly marriages, but thus far there are few on how to operate in a state of being a godly unmarried.

God's Word for the Unmarried Believer™ seeks to remind us that what His Word tells us is available to us whether or not a mate arrives.

We know there are many subjects and areas that are not specifically covered in this book. We couldn't do them all. But what we most want unmarrieds to know is that EVERY solution to EVERY question or problem that they may have is in the Bible.

God's Word provides comfort, direction, wholeness, promise, and fulfillment, with or without a mate. It is with this in mind that we present this book, first in a series that will include *Prayers for the Unmarried Believer*™ and *Devotions for the Unmarried Believer*™.

And for those of us who want to be married and

are still waiting for God's best for our lives in a mate, it is our prayer that this little book, filled with words of Life, will encourage you to spend your unmarried season, with all of its tears and joys, seeking first Him and His perfect will in all that you do.

THE EDITORS

God's Word
for the
Unmarried Believer™

Accountability

*You may think you are free, but you are still
accountable to God.*

* * *

GIRLFRIENDS BEV AND JOANNIE sat in aston-
ishment, their eyes glued to the television screen
as they watched the drama on a TV talk show play out
in front of them.

"Why would she tell that now after all of these
years," Bev wondered in disbelief. "I mean, no one
knew but her. Why couldn't she keep it to herself? Here
she is on *The Shame Show* and now everybody knows
her business."

"Yeah," said Joannie. "Some things you just don't
let anybody else know."

As unmarrieds we sometimes act as if we live
nonaccountable lives. We have no husbands, wives, or
kids to whom we either report our deeds and plans
or who find them out by snooping in our secret stuff.

But even when there is never a word spoken, never a journal page invaded, God always knows.

And while we know that God is in the love business and not the throw-it-up-in-your-face business, we would be wise to remember that there is *always* a witness—a Holy God—who expects and strengthens us to live in a manner than glorifies Him.

I will instruct thee and teach thee in the way which thou shalt go: I will guide thee with mine eye.

PSALMS 32:8

*B*ut if from thence thou shalt seek the LORD thy God, thou shalt find him, if thou seek him with all thy heart and with all thy soul.

DEUTERONOMY 4:29

*T*his book of the law shall not depart of thy mouth; but thou shalt meditate therein day and night, that thou mayest observe to do according to all that is written therein: for then thou shalt make thy way prosperous, and then thou shalt have good success.

JOSHUA 1:8

*B*e ye strong therefore, and let not your hands be weak: for your work shall be rewarded.

2 CHRONICLES 15:7

*B*ut his delight is in the law of the LORD; and in his law doth he meditate day and night.

PSALMS 1:2

*C*ounsel is mine, and sound wisdom: I am understanding; I have strength.

PROVERBS 8:14

*S*eek ye the LORD while he may be found, call ye upon him while he is near:

ISAIAH 55:6

*B*e careful for nothing; but in every thing by prayer and supplication with thanksgiving let your requests be made known to God.

PHILIPPIANS 4:6

*P*raying always with all prayer and supplication in the Spirit, and watching thereunto with all perseverance and supplication for all saints;

EPHESIANS 6:18

$\mathcal{I}$ exhort therefore, that, first of all, supplications, prayers, intercessions, and giving thanks, be made for all men;

For kings, and for all that are in authority; that we may lead a quiet and peaceable life in all godliness and honesty;

For this is good and acceptable in the sight of God our Saviour;

1 TIMOTHY 2:1–3

$\mathcal{A}$nd that servant, which knew his lord's will, and prepared not himself, neither did according to his will, shall be beaten with many stripes.

But he that knew not, and did commit things worthy of stripes, shall be beaten with few stripes. For unto whomsoever much is given, of him shall be much required: and to whom men have committed much, of him they will ask the more.

LUKE 12:47–48

$\mathcal{T}$rust ye in the LORD for ever: for in the LORD JEHO-VAH is everlasting strength:

ISAIAH 26:4

*A*nd when thou prayest, thou shalt not be as the hypocrites are: for they love to pray standing in the synagogues and in the corners of the streets, that they may be seen of men. Verily I say unto you, They have their reward.

But thou, when thou prayest, enter into thy closet, and when thou hast shut thy door, pray to thy Father which is in secret; and thy Father which seeth in secret shall reward thee openly.

But when ye pray, use not vain repetitions, as the heathen do: for they think that they shall be heard for their much speaking.

Be not ye therefore like unto them: for your Father knoweth what things ye have need of, before ye ask him.

MATTHEW 6:5–8

*B*lessed are the peacemakers: for they shall be called the children of God.

MATTHEW 5:9

O generation of vipers, how can ye, being evil, speak good things? For out of the abundance of the heart the mouth speaketh.

MATTHEW 12:34

But I say unto you, That every idle word that men shall speak, they shall give account thereof in the day of judgment.

For by thy words thou shalt be justified, and by thy words thou shalt be condemned.

MATTHEW 12:36–37

His lord said unto him, Well done, thou good and faithful servant: thou hast been faithful over a few things, I will make thee ruler over many things: enter thou into the joy of thy lord.

MATTHEW 25:21

Pray without ceasing.

In every thing give thanks: for this is the will of God in Christ Jesus concerning you. . . .

Prove all things; hold fast that which is good.

Abstain from all appearance of evil.

1 THESSALONIANS 5:17–18, 21–22

Anger

Get over it!

"I WAS SO MAD I couldn't even see straight."

Have you ever heard that before? Been there?

Most of us have. And as unmarrieds we sometimes feel that we have to fight every battle for ourselves. After all, who will take care of this situation if I don't? Who will get those people straight if I don't? Who will take up for me if I don't?

News flash! God will.

God knows better than anyone what we need and is more than capable of defending and protecting us against anything.

So let's not get mad. Let's get prayerful and tell God exactly how we feel about the situation. Let's tell Him why we are so angry and that we sincerely want the solution to come from Him rather than from ourselves.

Then let's listen to him. It is marvelous how God

can always find a peaceful and far less angry way to solve any problem we give Him.

The LORD shall fight for you and ye shall hold your peace.

EXODUS 14:14

Thy word have I hid in mine heart, that I might not sin against thee.

PSALMS 119:11

Great peace have they which love thy law: and nothing shall offend them.

PSALMS 119:165

Keep thy tongue from evil, and thy lips from speaking guile.

PSALMS 34:13

Cease from anger, and forsake wrath: fret not thyself in any wise to do evil.

PSALMS 37:8

Set a watch, O LORD, before my mouth; keep the door of my lips.

PSALMS 141:3

This is the day which the LORD hath made, we will rejoice and be glad in it.

PSALMS 118:24

Behold, thou desirest truth in the inward parts: and in the hidden part thou shalt make me know wisdom.

PSALMS 51:6

Create in me a clean heart, O GOD; and renew a right spirit within me.

PSALMS 51:10

A brother offended is harder to be won than a strong city: and their contentions are like the bars of a castle.

PROVERBS 18:19

The spirit of a man will sustain his infirmity; but a wounded spirit who can bear?

PROVERBS 18:14

The discretion of a man deferreth his anger; and it is his glory over a transgression.

PROVERBS 19:11

He that is slow to anger is better than the mighty; and he that ruleth his spirit than he that taketh a city.

PROVERBS 16:32

$\mathcal{A}$ soft answer turneth away wrath: but grievous words stir up anger.

PROVERBS 15:1

$\mathcal{A}$ wrathful man stirreth up strife: but he that is slow to anger appeaseth strife.

PROVERBS 15:18

$\mathcal{W}$hoso keepeth his mouth and his tongue keepeth his soul from troubles.

PROVERBS 21:23

$\mathcal{S}$he openeth her mouth with wisdom; and her tongue is the law of kindness.

PROVERBS 31:26

$\mathcal{B}$etter is the end of a thing than the beginning thereof: and the patient in spirit is better than the proud of spirit.

Be not hasty in thy spirit to be angry: for anger resteth in the bosom of fools.

ECCLESIASTES 7:8–9

$\mathcal{O}$ generation of vipers, how can ye, being evil, speak good things? For out of the abundance of the heart the mouth speaketh.

A good man out of the good treasure of the heart

bringeth forth good things: and an evil man out of the evil treasure bringeth forth evil things.

But I say unto you, That every idle word that men shall speak, they shall give account thereof in the day of judgment.

For by thy words thou shalt be justified, and by thy words thou shalt be condemned.

MATTHEW 12:34–37

Blessed are the peacemakers: for they shall be called the children of God.

MATTHEW 5:9

And when ye stand praying, forgive, if ye have ought against any: that your Father also which is in heaven may forgive you your trespasses.

But if ye do not forgive, neither will your Father which is in heaven forgive your trespasses.

MARK 11:25–26

So then they that are in the flesh cannot please God.

ROMANS 8:8

Dearly beloved, avenge not yourselves, but rather give place unto wrath: for it is written, Vengeance is mine; I will repay, saith the Lord.

ROMANS 12:19

*N*ow I beseech you, brethren, by the name of our Lord Jesus Christ, that ye all speak the same thing, and that there be no divisions among you; but that ye be perfectly joined together in the same mind and in the same judgment.

1 CORINTHIANS 1:10

*T*herefore if any man be in Christ, he is a new creature: old things are passed away; behold, all things are become new.

2 CORINTHIANS 5:17

*F*or though we walk in the flesh, we do not war after the flesh:

(For the weapons of our warfare are not carnal, but mighty through God to the pulling down of strong holds;)

Casting down imaginations, and every high thing that exalteth itself against the knowledge of God, and bringing into captivity every thought to the obedience of Christ;

2 CORINTHIANS 10:3-5

*I*dolatry, witchcraft, hatred, variance, emulations, wrath, strife, seditions, heresies,

Envying, murders, drunkenness, revellings, and such like: of which I tell you before, as I have also told you in time past, that they which do such things shall not inherit the kingdom of God.

But the fruit of the Spirit is love, joy, peace, long-suffering, gentleness, goodness, faith,

Meekness, temperance: against such there is no law.

And they that are Christ's have crucified the flesh with the affections and lusts.

If we live in the Spirit, let us also walk in the Spirit.

GALATIANS 5:20–26

Be ye angry, and sin not: let not the sun go down upon your wrath:

Neither give place to the devil.

EPHESIANS 4:26–27

Let no corrupt communication proceed out of your mouth, but that which is good to use of edifying, that it may minister grace unto the hearers.

And grieve not the Holy Spirit of God, whereby ye are sealed unto the day of redemption.

Let all bitterness, and wrath, and anger, and clamour, and evil speaking, be put away from you, with all malice:

And be ye kind one to another, tenderhearted, forgiving one another, even as God for Christ's sake hath forgiven you.

EPHESIANS 4:29–32

*B*ut speaking the truth in love, may grow up into him in all things, which is the head, even Christ:

EPHESIANS 4:15

*F*inally, brethren, whatsoever things are true, whatsoever things are honest, whatsoever things are just, whatsoever things are pure, whatsoever things are lovely, whatsoever things are of good report; if there be any virtue, and if there be any praise, think on these things.

PHILIPPIANS 4:8

*D*o all things without murmurings and disputings:

PHILIPPIANS 2:14

*R*ejoice in the Lord alway: and again I say, Rejoice.

PHILIPPIANS 4:4

*L*et the word of Christ dwell in you richly in all wisdom; teaching and admonishing one another in psalms and hymns and spiritual songs, singing with grace in your hearts to the Lord.

And whatsoever ye do in word or deed, do all in the name of the Lord Jesus, giving thanks to God and the Father by him.

COLOSSIANS 3:16–17

*S*ee that none render evil for evil unto any man; but ever follow that which is good, both among yourselves, and to all men.

1 THESSALONIANS 5:15

*A*nd the servant of the Lord must not strive; but be gentle unto all men, apt to teach, patient,

In meekness instructing those that oppose themselves; if God peradventure will give them repentance to the acknowledge of the truth;

And that they may recover themselves out of the snare of the devil, who are taken captive by him at his will.

2 TIMOTHY 2:24–26

*S*ubmit yourselves therefore to God. Resist the devil, and he will flee from you.

JAMES 4:7

*B*ut the wisdom that is from above is first pure, then peaceable, gentle, and easy to be intreated, full of mercy and fruits, with partiality, and without hypocrisy.

And the fruit of righteousness is sown in peace of them that make peace.

JAMES 3:17–18

Not rendering evil for evil, or railing for railing: but contrariwise blessing; knowing that ye are thereunto called, that ye should inherit a blessing.

1 PETER 3:9

Brokenhearted

Let God mend it.

DEBBIE FELT LIKE she was going to die. She had recently lost both of her parents and her three-year-old son in a tragic car accident.

Unmarried and an only child, she felt that there was no one who could possibly understand her pain.

"It hurt so bad," she says, "that my chest actually ached. I believed for a long time that I would never, ever, ever not have that pain."

But what Debbie learned one day in prayer was something that changed her forever.

"I was praying one morning just like I had done for years, but this time I stopped praying *about* my pain and for the first time I really thought about the fact He has sent Jesus to bear my grief and my pain, and I began to thank Him for what He had already done. Then I asked Him to restore me to the productive life I had before I lost my parents and my son.

"Immediately, it seemed like a blanket was lifted off of my shoulders," she said. "Then, slowly, I noticed creativity, energy, and my laughter begin to return to my life. I still miss my parents and my son—I think about them every day—but God has done a new thing in me. He mended a heart that I thought was irreparable."

Nothing is too difficult for God, and He has already made a way of soothing no matter how deep our pain and grief. He is the healer of your heart.

Now thanks be unto God, which always causeth us to triumph in Christ, and maketh manifest the savour of his knowledge by us in every place.

2 CORINTHIANS 2:14

We are troubled on every side, yet not distressed; we are perplexed, but not in despair;

Persecuted, but not forsaken; cast down, but not destroyed;

2 CORINTHIANS 4:8–9

For which cause we faint not; but though our outward man perish, yet the inward man is renewed day by day.

2 CORINTHIANS 4:16

The righteous cry, and the LORD heareth, and delivereth them out of all their troubles.

The LORD is nigh unto them that are of a broken heart; and saveth such as be of a contrite spirit.

Many are the afflictions of the righteous: but the LORD delivereth him out of them all.

PSALMS 34:17–19

The LORD shall preserve thee from all evil: he shall preserve thy soul.

The LORD shall preserve thy going out and thy coming in from this time forth, and even for evermore.

PSALMS 121:7–8

Though I walk in the midst of trouble, thou wilt revive me: thou shalt stretch forth thine hand against the wrath of mine enemies, and thy right hand shall save me.

PSALMS 138:7

Why art thou cast down, O my soul? and why art thou disquieted within me? hope in God: for I shall yet praise him, who is the health of my countenance, and my God.

PSALMS 43:5

Turn thee unto me, and have mercy upon me; for I am desolate and afflicted.

The troubles of my heart are enlarged: O bring thou me out of my distresses.

PSALMS 25:16–17

God is our refuge and strength, a very present help in trouble.

PSALMS 46:1

For whatsoever is born of God overcometh the world: and this is the victory that overcometh the world, even our faith.

Who is he that overcometh the world, but he that believeth that Jesus is the Son of God?

1 JOHN 5:4–5

Wherefore seeing we also are compassed about with so great a cloud of witnesses, let us lay aside every weight, and the sin which doth so easily beset us, and let us run with patience the race that is set before us,

HEBREWS 12:1

Blessed are ye that hunger now: for ye shall be filled. Blessed are ye that weep now: for ye shall laugh.

LUKE 6:21

Let not your heart be troubled: ye believe in God, believe also in me.

JOHN 14:1

Peace I leave with you, my peace I give unto you: not as the world giveth, give I unto you. Let not your heart be troubled, neither let it be afraid.

JOHN 14:27

And the peace of God, which passeth all understanding, shall keep your hearts and minds through Christ Jesus.

Finally, brethren, whatsoever things are true, whatsoever things are honest, whatsoever things are just, whatsoever things are pure, whatsoever things are lovely, whatsoever things are of good report; if there be any virtue, and if there be any praise, think on these things.

PHILIPPIANS 4:7–8

Deliver me, O LORD, from the evil man: preserve me from the violent man;

Which imagine mischiefs in their heart; continually are they gathered together for war.

PSALMS 140:1–2

He will not suffer thy foot to be moved: he that keepeth thee will not slumber.

PSALMS 121:3

Though he fall, he shall not be utterly cast down: for the LORD upholdeth him with his hand.

PSALMS 37:24

I cried unto thee, O LORD: I said, Thou art my refuge and my portion in the land of the living.

Attend unto my cry; for I am brought very low: deliver me from my persecutors; for they are stronger than I.

Bring my soul out of prison, that I may praise thy name: the righteous shall compass me about; for thou shalt deal bountifully with me.

PSALMS 142:5–7

My flesh and my heart faileth: but God is the strength of my heart, and my portion for ever.

PSALMS 73:26

Hope deferred maketh the heart sick: but when the desire cometh, it is a tree of life.

PROVERBS 13:12

Every word of God is pure: he is a shield unto them that put their trust in him.

PROVERBS 30:5

But if the Spirit of him that raised up Jesus from the dead dwell in you, he that raised up Christ from the dead shall also quicken your mortal bodies by his Spirit that dwelleth in you.

ROMANS 8:11

*A*nd it shall come to pass, that before they call, I will answer; and while they are yet speaking, I will hear.

ISAIAH 65:24

*F*ear thou not; for I am with thee: be not dismayed; for I am thy God: I will strengthen thee; yea, I will help thee; yea I will uphold thee with the right hand of my righteousness.

ISAIAH 41:10

*C*all unto me, and I will answer thee, and shew thee great and mighty things, which thou knowest not.

JEREMIAH 33:3

I will seek that which was lost, and bring again that which was driven away, and will bind up that which was broken, and will strengthen that which was sick: but I will destroy the fat and the strong; I will feed them with judgment.

EZEKIEL 34:16

Comfort

Ah, to rest in His arms.

IT WAS BACK.

It was four o'clock in the morning and Diann had been up all night. She had troubles. Job troubles. Man troubles. Health troubles. And, as it had been for years when troubles called her, sleeplessness answered.

It was too late to call her girlfriends, and she had read every Scripture she could find pertaining to her problems. Still, she was restless and wide awake.

As she watched the clock, her mind began to drift to a teaching she had heard at her church several months ago.

There, the singles' minister had encouraged the unmarrieds to seek comfort in the Holy Spirit rather than in other people.

She thought about what would really make her feel better right then and realized that although the things that were keeping her awake would take some effort on her part to fix, the comfort of a big hug from someone she knew loved her would go a long way toward making her at least *feel* better.

Then Diann closed her eyes and imagined the arms of the Almighty God enfolding her, holding her, and telling her that He was always there for her. Slowly, she began to sense the love of God enfolding her.

And there in His arms Diann rested. And she slept.

And he said, My presence shall go with thee, and I will give thee rest.

Exodus 33:14

Come unto me, all ye that labour and are heavy laden, and I will give you rest.

Take my yoke upon you, and learn of me; for I am meek and lowly in heart: and ye shall find rest unto your souls.

For my yoke is easy, and my burden is light.

Matthew 11:28–30

The Lord lift up his countenance upon thee, and give thee peace.

Numbers 6:26

℉or with God nothing shall be impossible.

LUKE 1:37

℉or God hath not given us the spirit of fear; but of power, and of love, and of a sound mind.

2 TIMOTHY 1:7

𝒦eep me as the apple of the eye, hide me under the shadow of thy wings,

PSALMS 17:8

ℋe that dwelleth in the secret place of the most High shall abide under the shadow of the Almighty.

I will say of the LORD, He is my refuge and my fortress: my God; in him will I trust.

Surely he shall deliver thee from the snare of the fowler, and from the noisome pestilence.

He shall cover thee with his feathers, and under his wings shalt thou trust: his truth shall be thy shield and buckler.

Thou shalt not be afraid for the terror by night; nor for the arrow that flieth by day;

Nor for the pestilence that walketh in darkness; nor for the destruction that wasteth at noonday.

A thousand shall fall at thy side, and ten thousand at thy right hand; but it shall not come nigh thee.

Only with thine eyes shalt thou behold and see the reward of the wicked.

Because thou hast made the LORD, which is my refuge, even the most High, thy habitation;

There shall no evil befall thee, neither shall any plague come nigh thy dwelling.

For he shall give his angels charge over thee, to keep thee in all thy ways.

They shall bear thee up in their hands, lest thou dash thy foot against a stone.

Thou shalt tread upon the lion and adder: the young lion and the dragon shalt thou trample under feet.

Because he hath set his love upon me, therefore will I deliver him: I will set him on high, because he hath known my name.

He shall call upon me, and I will answer him: I will be with him in trouble; I will deliver him, and honour him.

With long life will I satisfy him, and shew him my salvation.

PSALMS 91:1–16

Wait on the LORD: be of good courage, and he shall strengthen thine heart: wait, I say, on the LORD.

PSALMS 27:14

Be of good courage, and he shall strengthen your heart, all ye that hope in the LORD.

PSALMS 31:24

The angel of the LORD encampeth round about them that fear him, and delivereth them.

PSALMS 34:7

I laid me down and slept; I awakened; for the LORD sustained me.

I will not be afraid of ten thousands of people, that have set themselves against me round about.

PSALMS 3:5–6

Trust in the LORD with all thine heart; and lean not unto thine own understanding.

In all thy ways acknowledge him, and he shall direct thy paths.

PROVERBS 3:5–6

For the LORD shall be thy confidence, and shall keep thy foot from being taken.

PROVERBS 3:26

And in that day ye shall ask me nothing. Verily, verily, I say unto you, Whatsoever ye shall ask the Father in my name, he will give it you.

JOHN 16:23

If the world hate you, ye know that it hated me before it hated you.

If ye were of the world, the world would love his

own: but because ye are not of the world, but I have chosen you out of the world, therefore the world hateth you.

JOHN 15:18–19

*A*nd I will pray the Father, and he shall give you another Comforter, that he may abide with you for ever;

Even the Spirit of truth; whom the world cannot receive, because it seeth him not, neither knoweth him: but ye know him; for he dwelleth with you, and shall be in you.

I will not leave you comfortless: I will come to you.

JOHN 14:16–18

*F*or I am persuaded, that neither death, nor life, nor angels, nor principalities, nor powers, nor things present, nor things to come,

Nor height, nor depth, nor any other creature, shall be able to separate us from the love of God, which is in Christ Jesus our Lord.

ROMANS 8:38–39

*A*nd the God of peace shall bruise Satan under your feet shortly. The grace of our Lord Jesus Christ be with you. Amen.

ROMANS 16:20

Wherefore seeing we also are compassed about with so great a cloud of witnesses, let us lay aside every weight, and the sin which doth so easily beset us, and let us run with patience the race that is set before us,

Looking unto Jesus the author and finisher of our faith; who for the joy that was set before him endured the cross, despising the shame, and is set down at the right hand of the throne of God.

HEBREWS 12:1-2

For all the promises of God in him are yea, and in him Amen, unto the glory of God by us.

2 CORINTHIANS 1:20

Casting all your care upon him; for he careth for you.

1 PETER 5:7

But and if ye suffer for righteousness' sake, happy are ye: and be not afraid of their terror, neither be troubled;

1 PETER 3:14

Having a good conscience; that, whereas they speak evil of you, as of evildoers, they may be ashamed that falsely accuse your good conversation in Christ.

For it is better, if the will of God be so, that ye suffer for well doing, than for evil doing.

1 PETER 3:16-17

And whatsoever we ask, we receive of him, because we keep his commandments, and do those things that are pleasing in his sight.

1 JOHN 3:22

Fear thou not; for I am with thee: be not dismayed; for I am thy God: I will strengthen thee; yea, I will help thee; yea, I will uphold thee with the right hand of my righteousness.

ISAIAH 41:10

Thou wilt keep him in perfect peace, whose mind is stayed on thee: because he trusteth in thee.

ISAIAH 26:3

Finally, my brethren, be strong in the Lord, and in the power of his might.

EPHESIANS 6:10

Wherefore take unto you the whole armour of God, that ye may be able to withstand in the evil day, and having done all, to stand.

Stand therefore, having your loins girt about with truth, and having on the breastplate of righteousness;

And your feet shod with the preparation of the gospel of peace;

Above all, taking the shield of faith, wherewith ye shall be able to quench all the fiery darts of the wicked.

And take the helmet of salvation, and the sword of the Spirit, which is the word of God:

EPHESIANS 6:13-17

$\mathcal{I}$ can do all things through Christ which strengtheneth me.

PHILIPPIANS 4:13

Confidence

*It doesn't matter who you think you are,
only who God says you are.*

"I HAD JUST STARTED my own business," said
Stephen, a successful entrepreneur, "and I met a really
nice woman who was an accounting wiz. She was attractive and went to my church. Numbers had never been
my personal strong suit, so I thought, Hey maybe this is
the woman God is sending me as my helpmeet.

"We dated for about six months and her accounting skills were a tremendous blessing to me. But what
blessed me more was that each time I told her I did not
have the brains for numbers, she would encourage me
by telling me that God would not have given me such a
wonderful idea for a business and then leave me brain-
dead when it came to the financial part. She even typed
up some Scriptures and encouraged me to meditate on
them.

"I got bold, sent off for a few catalogs, and enrolled in some accounting classes at the local community college. Me and Holy Spirit aced every course! Now I volunteer with a Christian businesspersons' network mentoring others. My specialty? Accounting for small businesses!"

"Even though our dating relationship didn't work out, that Sister was a blessing to me because she didn't try to puff me up with her own opinions but instead pointed me in the direction of The Word and what God says about me."

We can count on God when we can't count on ourselves.

※

*A*nd let us not be weary in well doing: for in due season we shall reap, if we faint not.

GALATIANS 6:9

*H*ave not I commanded thee? Be strong and of a good courage; be not afraid, neither be thou dismayed: for the LORD thy God is with thee whithersoever thou goest.

JOSHUA 1:9

*F*or God hath not given us the spirit of fear; but of power, and of love, and of a sound mind.

2 TIMOTHY 1:7

So shall my word be that goeth forth out of my mouth: it shall not return unto me void, but it shall accomplish that which I please, and it shall prosper in the thing whereto I sent it.

ISAIAH 55:11

Fear thou not: for I am with thee: be not dismayed; for I am thy God: I will strengthen thee; yea, I will help thee; yea, I will uphold thee with the right hand of my righteousness.

ISAIAH 41:10

For I the LORD thy God will hold thy right hand, saying unto thee, Fear not; I will help thee.

ISAIAH 41:13

There was a certain rich man, which was clothed in purple and fine linen, and fared sumptuously every day:

LUKE 16:19

Who his own self bare our sins in his own body on the tree, that we, being dead to sins, should live unto righteousness: by whose stripes ye were healed.

1 PETER 2:24

And ye shall serve the Lord your god, and he shall bless thy bread, and thy water; and I will take sickness away from the midst of thee.

EXODUS 23:25

Come unto me, all ye that labour and are heavy laden, and I will give you rest.

MATTHEW 11:28

Be careful for nothing; but in every thing by prayer and supplication with thanksgiving let your requests be made known unto God.

And the peace of God, which passeth all understanding, shall keep your hearts and minds through Christ Jesus.

PHILIPPIANS 4:6-7

Be strong and of good courage, fear not, nor be afraid of them: for the Lord thy God, he it is that doth go with thee; he will not fail thee, nor forsake thee.

DEUTERONOMY 31:6

And this is the confidence that we have in him, that, if we ask any thing according to his will, he heareth us:

And if we know that he hear us, whatsoever we

ask, we know that we have the petitions that we desired of him.

1 JOHN 5:14-15

Beloved, if our heart condemn us not, then have we confidence toward God.

And whatsoever we ask, we receive of him, because we keep his commandments, and do those things that are pleasing in his sight.

1 JOHN 3:21-22

The young lions do lack, and suffer hunger; but they that seek the LORD shall not want any good thing.

PSALMS 34:10

Commit thy way unto the LORD; trust also in him; and he shall bring it to pass.

PSALMS 37:5

Trust in him at all times; ye people, pour out your heart before him: God is a refuge for us. Selah.

PSALMS 62:8

Cast thy burden upon the LORD, and he shall sustain thee: he shall never suffer the righteous to be moved.

PSALMS 55:22

But thou, O Lord, art a shield for me; my glory, and the lifter up of mine head.

PSALMS 3:3

What shall we then say to these things? If God be for us, who can be against us?

ROMANS 8:31

There is therefore now no condemnation to them which are in Christ Jesus, who walk not after the flesh, but after the Spirit.

ROMANS 8:1

For the law of the Spirit of life in Christ Jesus hath made me free from the law of sin and death.

ROMANS 8:2

But if the Spirit of him that raised up Jesus from the dead dwell in you, he that raised up Christ from the dead shall also quicken your mortal bodies by his Spirit that dwelleth in you.

ROMANS 8:11

For I am persuaded, that neither death, nor life, nor angels, nor principalities, nor powers, nor things present, nor things to come,

Nor height, nor depth, nor any other creature,

shall be able to separate us from the love of God, which is in Christ Jesus our Lord.

ROMANS 8:38–39

This I recall to my mind, therefore I have hope.

It is of the LORD'S mercies that we are not consumed, because his compassions fail not.

They are new every morning: great is thy faithfulness.

The LORD is my portion, saith my soul; therefore will I hope in him.

LAMENTATIONS 3:21–24

But the Lord is faithful, who shall establish you, and keep you from evil.

2 THESSALONIANS 3:3

For all the promises of God in him are yea, and in him Amen, unto the glory of God by us.

2 CORINTHIANS 1:20

In that day it shall be said to Jerusalem, Fear thou not: and to Zion, Let not thine hands be slack.

ZEPHANIAH 3:16

Cast not away therefore your confidence, which hath great recompence of reward.

For ye have need of patience, that, after ye have done the will of God, ye might receive the promise.

Hebrews 10:35–36

Jesus Christ the same yesterday, and to day, and for ever.

Hebrews 13:8

Trust in the LORD with all thine heart; and lean not unto thine own understanding.

Proverbs 3:5

For the LORD shall be thy confidence, and shall keep thy foot from being taken.

Proverbs 3:26

For I know the thoughts that I think toward you, saith the LORD, thoughts of peace, and not of evil, to give you an expected end.

Jeremiah 29:11

And yet if I judge, my judgment is true: for I am not alone, but I and the Father that sent me.

John 8:16

Behold, the hour cometh, yea, is now come, that ye shall be scattered, every man to his own, and shall leave me alone: and yet I am not alone, because the Father is with me.

JOHN 16:32

And he that sent me is with me: the Father hath not left me alone; for I do always those things that please him.

JOHN 8:29

Confusion

Feeling pulled in a bunch of different directions? The one that leads to Him is the way.

WE'VE ALL HEARD IT a million times: "God is not the author of confusion."

When we feel like we are being torn in a thousand directions and find ourselves not being able to make a decision, there is really only one thing we need to make up our mind to put into action—prayer.

God is not holding information back from us, and it is not written in secret code. He wants to give us what we need, and prayer is the key to pulling back the curtain on confusion.

When you're feeling undecided and confused, spend more time with Him and in prayer. There are solutions you never dreamed of at the feet of the Father!

Follow peace with all men, and holiness, without which no man shall see the Lord:

Looking diligently lest any man fail of the grace of God; lest any root of bitterness springing up trouble you, and thereby many be defiled;

HEBREWS 12:14–15

In the multitude of my thoughts within me thy comforts delight my soul.

PSALMS 94:19

God is our refuge and strength, a very present help in trouble.

Therefore will not we fear, though the earth be removed, and though the mountains be carried into the midst of the sea;

Though the waters thereof roar and be troubled, though the mountains shake with the swelling thereof. Selah.

PSALMS 46:1–3

Let this mind be in you, which was also in Christ Jesus.

PHILIPPIANS 2:5

For God is not the author of confusion, but of peace, as in all churches of the saints.

1 CORINTHIANS 14:33

Commit thy works unto the LORD, and thy thoughts shall be established.

PROVERBS 16:3

Casting down imaginations, and every high thing that exalteth itself against the knowledge of God, and bringing into captivity every thought to the obedience of Christ;

2 CORINTHIANS 10:5

And the peace of God, which passeth all understanding, shall keep your hearts and minds through Christ Jesus.

Finally, brethren, whatsoever things are true, whatsoever things are honest, whatsoever things are just, whatsoever things are pure, whatsoever things are lovely, whatsoever things are of good report; if there be any virtue, and if there be any praise, think on these things.

PHILIPPIANS 4:7–8

Thou wilt keep him in perfect peace, whose mind is stayed on thee: because he trusteth in thee.

ISAIAH 26:3

But thou, O LORD, art a shield for me; my glory, and the lifter up of mine head.

PSALMS 3:3

Wait on the Lord: be of good courage, and he shall strengthen thine heart: wait, I say, on the Lord.

PSALMS 27:14

Contentment

That's satisfaction.

IF ONLY I HAD ...
   If only I had known ...
   If only I were ...
   Most all of us could spend days filling in *those* blanks!
   Instead, why not spend a minute filling in these?
   I am glad I understand ...
   I'm so thankful I know ...
   I believe I can ...

*L*et your conversation be without covetousness; and be content with such things as ye have: for he hath said, I will never leave thee, nor forsake thee.

HEBREWS 13:5

And let the peace of God rule in your hearts, to the which also ye are called in one body; and be ye thankful.

COLOSSIANS 3:15-16

They that trust in the LORD shall be as mount Zion, which cannot be removed, but abideth for ever.

As the mountains are round about Jerusalem, so the LORD is round about his people from henceforth even for ever.

PSALMS 125:1-2

Thou wilt keep him in perfect peace, whose mind is stayed on thee: because he trusteth in thee.

Trust ye in the LORD for ever: for in the LORD JEHOVAH is everlasting strength:

ISAIAH 26:3-4

To every thing there is a season, and a time to every purpose under the heaven:

ECCLESIASTES 3:1

The LORD lift up his countenance upon thee, and give thee peace.

NUMBERS 6:26

Be confident of this very thing, that he which hath begun a good work in you will perform it until the day of Jesus Christ:

PHILIPPIANS 1:6

Let us therefore follow after the right things which make for peace, and things wherewith one may edify another.

ROMANS 14:19

For this God is our God for ever and ever: he will be our guide even unto death.

PSALMS 48:14

That your faith should not stand in the wisdom of men, but in the power of God.

1 CORINTHIANS 2:5

A time to weep, and a time to laugh; a time to mourn, and a time to dance;

ECCLESIASTES 3:4

A time to get, and a time to lose; a time to keep, and a time to cast away;

ECCLESIASTES 3:6

The LORD will give strength unto his people; the LORD will bless his people with peace.

PSALMS 29:11

Not that I speak in respect of want: for I have learned, in whatsoever state I am, therewith to be content.

I know both how to be abased, and I know how to abound: every where and in all things I am instructed both to be full and to be hungry, both to abound and to suffer need.

I can do all things through Christ which strengtheneth me.

PHILIPPIANS 4:11–13

Disappointment

It happens to all of us.

SOMETIMES, no matter how hard we pray, things just don't work out the way we hope they will.

If we are not careful, disappointments, which are no more than preconceived notions that don't work out, will sidetrack us and take us down a path of self-pity and thanklessness.

It's okay to be sad, but the key is not to find your way into Disappointment Land and dwell too long. Not having a husband or a wife to cheer you up as if it were his or her part-time job is no excuse to wallow in your failures. God is *good*.

The next time things don't work out exactly as you planned, take five minutes and write down two things God *has* worked out, two things He *has* delivered, and one thing you promised *yourself* that you know He was good enough to give you the strength to finish.

Then draw yourself a new map. Use the Word of God as your compass and you will see that all roads lead to God's perfect will.

Make a decision to trade in that pain for the joy of the Lord!

✳

I wait for the LORD, my soul doth wait, and in his word do I hope.

PSALMS 130:5

*W*hy are thou cast down, O my soul? and why art thou disquieted within me? hope in God: for I shall yet praise him, who is the health of my countenance, and my God.

PSALMS 43:5

*F*or whatsoever is born of God overcometh the world: and this is the victory that overcometh the world, even our faith.

1 JOHN 5:4

*T*hen came Peter to him, and said, Lord, how oft shall my brother sin against me, and I forgive him? till seven times?

Jesus said unto him, I say not unto thee, Until seven times: but, Until seventy times seven.

MATTHEW 18:21-22

Be careful for nothing; but in every thing by prayer and supplication with thanksgiving let your requests be made known unto God.

PHILIPPIANS 4:6

And the peace of God, which passeth all understanding, shall keep your hearts and minds through Christ Jesus.

PHILIPPIANS 4:7

I can do all things through Christ which strengtheneth me.

PHILIPPIANS 4:13

Rest in the LORD, and wait patiently for him: fret not thyself because of him who prospereth in his way, because of the man who bringeth wicked devices to pass.

Cease from anger, and forsake wrath: fret not thyself in any wise to do evil.

PSALMS 37:7–8

Behold, the hour cometh, yea, is now come, that ye shall be scattered, every man to his own, and shall leave me alone: and yet I am not alone, because the Father is with me.

These things I have spoken unto you, that in me ye might have peace. In the world ye have tribulation: but be of good cheer; I have overcome the world.

JOHN 16:32–33

Casting all your care upon him; for he careth for you.

1 PETER 5:7

Now the God of hope fill you with all joy and peace in believing, that ye may abound in hope, through the power of the Holy Ghost.

ROMANS 15:13

It is better to trust in the LORD than to put confidence in man.

It is better to trust in the LORD than to put confidence in princes.

PSALMS 118:8–9

But I say unto you, Love your enemies, bless them that curse you, do good to them that hate you, and pray for them which despitefully use you, and persecute you;

MATTHEW 5:44

So that we may boldly say, The Lord is my helper, I will not fear what man shall do unto me.

HEBREWS 13:6

And the Lord turned the captivity of Job, when he prayed for his friends: also the Lord gave Job twice as much as he had before.

Job 42:10

So the Lord blessed the latter end of Job more than his beginning: for he had fourteen thousand sheep, six thousand camels, and a thousand yoke of oxen, and a thousand she asses.

Job 42:12

Divorce

God will hold your hand.

YOUR HEART IS BROKEN and, so you say, is your marriage.

Reach out and take hold of The One who says His hand will always be stretched toward you. He is your strength, your comfort, and your peace. No matter what it sounds like or looks like, or what it feels like, He is greatly to be praised!

When a man's ways please the LORD, he maketh even his enemies to be at peace with him.

PROVERBS 16:7

Brethren, I count not myself to have apprehended: but this one thing I do, forgetting those things which are behind, and reaching forth unto those things which are before,

I press toward the mark for the prize of the high calling of God in Christ Jesus.

PHILIPPIANS 3:13-14

Let this mind be in you, which is also in Christ Jesus:

PHILIPPIANS 2:5

And I will restore you the years that the locust hath eaten, the cankerworm, and the caterpiller, and the palmerworm, my great army which I sent among you.

And ye shall eat plenty, and be satisfied, and praise the name of the LORD your God, that hath dealt wondrously with you: and my people shall never be ashamed.

JOEL 2:25-26

Casting all your care upon him; for he careth for you.

Be sober, be vigilant; because your adversary the devil, as a roaring lion, walketh about, seeking whom he may devour:

1 PETER 5:7-8

And be ye kind one to another, tenderhearted, for-giving one another, even as God for Christ's sake hath forgiven you.

EPHESIANS 4:32

Be ye angry, and sin not: let not the sun go down upon your wrath: Neither give place to the devil.

EPHESIANS 4:26–27

And I will cleanse them from all their iniquity, whereby they have sinned against me; and I will pardon all their iniquities, whereby they have sinned, and whereby they have transgressed against me.

JEREMIAH 33:8

For I know the thoughts that I have toward you, saith the LORD, thoughts of peace, and not of evil, to give you an expected end.

Then shall ye call upon me, and ye shall go and pray unto me, and I will hearken unto you.

JEREMIAH 29:11–12

For if our heart condemn us, God is greater than our heart, and knoweth all things.

1 JOHN 3:20

We are troubled on every side, yet not distressed; we are perplexed, but not in despair;

Persecuted, but not forsaken; cast down, but not destroyed.

2 CORINTHIANS 4:8–9

$\mathcal{S}$eeing then that we have a great high priest, that is passed into the heavens, Jesus the Son of God, let us hold fast our profession.

For we have not an high priest which cannot be touched with the feeling of our infirmities; but was in all points tempted like as we are, yet without sin.

Let us therefore come boldly unto the throne of grace, that we may obtain mercy, and find grace to help in time of need.

HEBREWS 4:14-16

$\mathcal{F}$or the mountains shall depart, and the hills be removed; but my kindness shall not depart from thee, neither shall the covenant of my peace be removed, saith the LORD that hath mercy on thee.

ISAIAH 54:10

$\mathcal{N}$o weapon that is formed against thee shall prosper; and every tongue that shall rise against thee in judgment thou shalt condemn. This is the heritage of the servants of the LORD, and their righteousness is of me, saith the LORD.

ISAIAH 54:17

$\mathcal{I}$, even I, am he that blotteth out thy transgressions for mine own sake, and will not remember thy sins.

ISAIAH 43:25

To appoint unto them that mourn in Zion, to give unto them beauty for ashes, the oil of joy for mourning, the garment of praise for the spirit of heaviness; that they might be called trees of righteousness, the planting of the LORD, that he might be glorified.

ISAIAH 61:3

But if the unbelieving depart, let him depart. A brother or a sister is not under bondage in such cases; but God hath called us to peace.

1 CORINTHIANS 7:15

Have mercy upon me, O LORD, for I am in trouble: mine eye is consumed with grief, yea my soul and my belly.

PSALMS 31:9

For he shall deliver the needy when he crieth; the poor also, and him that hath no helper.

PSALMS 72:12

My soul, wait thou only upon God; for my expectation is from him.

He only is my rock and my salvation: he is my defence; I shall not be moved.

In God is my salvation and my glory: the rock of my strength, and my refuge, is in God.

PSALMS 62:5–7

Deliver me out of the mire, and let me not sink: let me be delivered from them that hate me, and out of the deep waters.

Let not the waterflood overflow me, neither let the deep swallow me up, and let not the pit shut her mouth upon me.

Hear me, O LORD: for thy lovingkindness is good: turn unto me according to the multitude of thy tender mercies.

And hide not thy face from thy servant; for I am in trouble: hear me speedily.

Draw nigh unto my soul, and redeem it: deliver me because of mine enemies.

PSALMS 69:14–18

See that none render evil for evil unto any man; but ever follow that which is good, both among yourselves, and to all men.

1 THESSALONIANS 5:15

And the voice spake unto him again the second time, What God hath cleansed, that call not thou common.

ACTS 10:15

And when ye stand praying, forgive, if ye have ought against any: that your Father also which is in heaven may forgive you your trespasses.

MARK 11:25

For if ye forgive men their trespasses, your heavenly Father will also forgive you:

But if ye forgive not men their trespasses, neither will your Father forgive your trespasses.

MATTHEW 6:14-15

But I say unto you, Love your enemies, bless them that curse you, do good to them that hate you, and pray for them which despitefully use you, and persecute you;

MATTHEW 5:44

Whom have I in heaven but thee? and there is none upon earth that I desire beside thee.

My flesh and my heart faileth: but God is the strength of my heart, and my portion for ever.

PSALMS 73:25-26

The LORD also will be a refuge for the oppressed, a refuge in times of trouble.

PSALMS 9:9

Now the God of hope fill you with all joy and peace in believing, that ye may abound in hope, through the power of the Holy Ghost.

ROMANS 15:13

Dearly beloved, avenge not yourselves, but rather give place unto wrath: for it is written, Vengeance is mine; I will repay, saith the Lord.

Therefore if thine enemy hunger, feed him; if he thirst, give him drink: for in so doing thou shalt heap coals of fire on his head.

Be not overcome of evil, but overcome evil with good.

ROMANS 12:19–21

When my father and my mother forsake me, then the LORD will take me up.

PSALMS 27:10

He healeth the broken in heart, and bindeth up their wounds.

PSALMS 147:3

The thief cometh not, but for to steal, and to kill, and to destroy: I am come that they might have life, and that they might have it more abundantly.

JOHN 10:10

When Jesus had lifted up himself, and saw none but the woman, he said unto her, Woman, where are those thine accusers? hath no man condemned thee?

She said, No man, Lord. And Jesus said unto her, Neither do I condemn thee: go, and sin no more.

JOHN 8:10–11

I will not leave you comfortless: I will come to you.

JOHN 14:18

For with God nothing shall be impossible.

LUKE 1:37

But I say unto you which hear, Love your enemies, do good to them which hate you,

Bless them that curse you, and pray for them which despitefully use you.

LUKE 6:27–28

O love the LORD, all ye his saints: for the LORD preserveth the faithful, and plentifully rewardeth the proud doer.

Be of good courage, and he shall strengthen your heart, all ye that hope in the LORD.

PSALMS 31:23–24

Lift up thyself, thou judge of the earth: render a reward to the proud.

PSALMS 94:2

The LORD is nigh unto them that are of a broken heart; and saveth such as be of a contrite spirit.

PSALMS 34:18

The eyes of the LORD are upon the righteous, and his ears are open unto their cry.

PSALMS 34:15

Entrepreneur

*You've already got the only partner
you'll ever need.*

MOST OF US SPEND OUR TIME lamenting what we don't know rather than thanking God because He knows everything!

Oftentimes in business, our fear of what we do not know, or have, causes us to "hook up" with those we think can fill those gaps, and we call them our partners.

Before you reach out to others, consider taking God on as your partner. He'll never blow a presentation, forget what He agreed to do, be late for a meeting, or vote you out!

With God as your partner, you can't help but succeed—in spite of yourself.

❋

A good man sheweth favour, and lendeth: he will guide his affairs with discretion.

Surely he shall not be moved for ever: the righteous shall be in everlasting remembrance.

He shall not be afraid of evil tidings: his heart is fixed, trusting in the LORD.

PSALMS 112:5–7

*H*e that hath clean hands, and a pure heart; who hath not lifted up his soul unto vanity, nor sworn deceitfully.

He shall receive the blessing from the LORD, and righteousness from the God of his salvation.

PSALMS 24:4–5

*T*each me thy way, O LORD, and lead me in a plain path, because of mine enemies.

PSALMS 27:11

*W*herefore be ye not unwise, but understanding what the will of the Lord is.

EPHESIANS 5:17

*C*asting all your care upon him; for he careth for you.

1 PETER 5:7

He becometh poor that dealeth with a slack hand: but the hand of the diligent maketh rich.

He that gathereth in summer is a wise son: but he that sleepeth in harvest is a son that causeth shame.

PROVERBS 10:4-5

The hand of the diligent shall bear rule: but the slothful shall be under tribute.

PROVERBS 12:24

The soul of the sluggard desireth, and hath nothing: but the soul of the diligent shall be made fat.

PROVERBS 13:4

Wealth gotten by vanity shall be diminished: but he that gathereth by labour shall increase.

PROVERBS 13:11

But my God shall supply all your need according to his riches in glory by Christ Jesus.

PHILIPPIANS 4:19

Masters, give unto your servants that which is just and equal; knowing that ye also have a Master in heaven.

COLOSSIANS 4:1

Remember ye not the former things, neither consider the things of old.

Behold, I will do a new thing; now it shall spring forth; shall ye not know it? I will even make a way in the wilderness, and rivers in the desert.

ISAIAH 43:18-19

Enlarge the place of thy tent, and let them stretch forth the curtains of thine habitations: spare not, lengthen thy cords, and strengthen thy stakes;

ISAIAH 54:2

Fear not; for thou shalt be not ashamed: neither be thou confounded; for thou shalt not be put to shame: for thou shalt forget the shame of thy youth, and shalt not remember the reproach of thy widowhood any more.

ISAIAH 54:4

For my thoughts are not your thoughts, neither are your ways my ways, saith the LORD.

For as the heavens are higher than the earth, so are my ways higher than your ways, and my thoughts than your thoughts.

ISAIAH 55:8-9

*M*oreover it is required in stewards, that a man be found faithful.

1 CORINTHIANS 4:2

*B*y humility and fear of the LORD are riches, and honour, and life.

PROVERBS 22:4

*S*eest thou a man diligent in his business? he shall stand before kings; he shall not stand before mean men.

PROVERBS 22:29

*L*ove not sleep, lest thou come to poverty; open thine eyes, and thou shalt be satisfied with bread.

PROVERBS 20:13

*D*ivers weights, and divers measures, both of them are alike abomination to the LORD.

PROVERBS 20:10

*H*umble yourselves in the sight of the Lord and he shall lift you up.

JAMES 4:10

Whatsoever thy hand findeth to do, do it with thy might; for there is no work, no device, nor knowledge, nor wisdom, in the grave, whither thou goest.

ECCLESIASTES 9:10

Except the LORD build the house, they labour in vain that build it: except the LORD keep the city, the watchman waketh but in vain.

PSALMS 127:1

I will instruct thee and teach thee in the way which thou shalt go: I will guide thee with mine eye.

PSALMS 32:8

And let the beauty of the LORD our God be upon us: and establish thou the work of our hands upon us; yea, the work of our hands establish thou it.

PSALMS 90:17

If it be possible, as much as lieth in you, live peaceably with all men.

ROMANS 12:18

Woe unto him that buildeth his house by unrighteousness, and his chambers by wrong; that useth his neighbour's service without wages, and giveth him not for his work;

JEREMIAH 22:13

$\mathcal{B}$e thou diligent to know the state of thy flocks, and look well to thy herds.

PROVERBS 27:23

$\mathcal{W}$hen the righteous are in authority, the people rejoice: but when the wicked beareth rule, the people mourn.

PROVERBS 29:2

$\mathcal{T}$rust in the LORD with all thine heart; and lean not unto thine own understanding.

In all thy ways acknowledge him, and he shall direct thy paths.

PROVERBS 3:5–6

$\mathcal{B}$ut there is a spirit in man: and the inspiration of the Almighty giveth them understanding.

JOB 32:8

$\mathcal{H}$e that is faithful in that which is least is faithful also in much: and he that is unjust in the least is unjust also in much.

If therefore ye have not been faithful in the unrighteous mammon, who will commit to your trust the true riches?

And if ye have not been faithful in that which is another man's, who shall give you that which is your own?

LUKE 16:10–12

The LORD bless thee, and keep thee:

The LORD make his face shine upon thee, and be gracious unto thee:

The LORD lift up his countenance upon thee, and give thee peace.

NUMBERS 6:24-26

And that ye study to be quiet, and to do your own business, and to work with your own hands, as we commanded you;

That ye may walk honestly toward them that are without, and that ye may have lack of nothing.

1 THESSALONIANS 4:11-12

That which is altogether just shalt thou follow, that thou mayest live, and inherit the land which the LORD thy God giveth thee.

DEUTERONOMY 16:20

And whosoever shall exalt himself shall be abased; and he that shall humble himself shall be exalted.

MATTHEW 23:12

But seek ye first the kingdom of God, and his righteousness; and all these things shall be added unto you.

MATTHEW 6:33

For even where we were with you, this we commanded you, that if any would not work, neither should he eat.

2 THESSALONIANS 3:10

Fantasies

Stop! You don't want to go there!

GOD HAS GIVEN US wonderful imaginations, but how we use them is up to us.

Think about it. When your mind wanders, is it toward lustful, sexy fantasies? Nothing wrong with that? Okay, then share them with the object of your thoughts.

When you get out of jail (why do you think personal protection orders reached an all-time high in this country last year?), realize that your thoughts are powerful, and, as an unmarried, your mind's fantasies are the first step in taking your body someplace you really, really may not want to go.

There's no easy way to do this. If you find yourself wandering into dangerous territory, *stop* and remind yourself that a Holy God created your imagination. Then begin to use it for something that glorifies its Maker!

We know that whosoever is born of God sinneth not; but he that is begotten of God keepeth himself, and that wicked one toucheth him not.

1 JOHN 5:18

For God hath not called us unto uncleanness, but unto holiness.

1 THESSALONIANS 4:7

Marriage is honourable in all, and the bed undefiled: but whoremongers and adulterers God will judge.

HEBREWS 13:4

But they that will be rich fall into temptation and a snare, and into many foolish and hurtful lusts, which drown men in destruction and perdition.

For the love of money is the root of all evil: which while some coveted after, they have erred from the faith, and pierced themselves through with many sorrows.

But thou, O man of God, flee these things; and follow after righteousness, godliness, faith, love, patience, meekness.

1 TIMOTHY 6:9–11

*K*now ye not that the unrighteous shall not inherit the kingdom of God? Be not deceived: neither fornicators, nor idolaters, nor adulterers, nor effeminate, nor abusers of themselves with mankind,

1 Corinthians 6:9

*F*lee fornication. Every sin that a man doeth is without the body; but he that committeth fornication sinneth against his own body.

What? know ye not that your body is the temple of the Holy Ghost which is in you, which ye have of God, and ye are not your own?

For ye are bought with a price: therefore glorify God in your body, and in your spirit, which are God's.

1 Corinthians 6:18–20

*B*ut whoso committeth adultery with a woman lacketh understanding: he that doeth it destroyeth his own soul.

Proverbs 6:32

*C*an a man take fire in his bosom, and his clothes not be burned?

Can one go upon hot coals, and his feet not be burned?

Proverbs 6:27–28

But I say unto you, That whosoever looketh on a woman to lust after her hath committed adultery with her already in his heart.

MATTHEW 5:28

For this is the will of God, even your sanctification, that ye should abstain from fornication:

That every one of you should know how to possess his vessel in sanctification and honour;

1 THESSALONIANS 4:3-4

Submit yourselves therefore to God. Resist the devil, and he will flee from you.

Draw nigh to God, and he will draw nigh to you. Cleanse your hands, ye sinners; and purify your hearts, ye double minded.

JAMES 4:7-8

Let this mind be in you, which was also in Christ Jesus:

PHILIPPIANS 2:5

Thy word have I hid in mine heart, that I might not sin against thee.

PSALMS 119:11

$\mathcal{F}$or he that soweth to his flesh shall of the flesh reap corruption; but he that soweth to the Spirit shall of the Spirit reap life everlasting.

GALATIANS 6:8

$\mathcal{F}$or we must all appear before the judgment seat of Christ; that every one may receive the things done in his body, according to that he hath done, whether it be good or bad.

2 CORINTHIANS 5:10

$\mathcal{S}$o then they that are in the flesh cannot please God.

ROMANS 8:8

$\mathcal{C}$asting down imaginations, and every high thing that exalteth itself against the knowledge of God, and bringing into captivity every thought to the obedience of Christ;

2 CORINTHIANS 10:5

$\mathcal{B}$ut I keep under my body, and bring it into subjection: lest that by any means, when I have preached to others, I myself should be a castaway.

1 CORINTHIANS 9:27

Fear

No need to be stressed—you're too blessed!

YOU KNOW WHAT you *want* to do, and you know what you *should* do.

You know what you would like to happen, but suppose it doesn't?

The stress is unbearable. You need to do something. Decisions need to be made.

Fear. Fear of being wrong. Fear of being right. Fear of making the wrong decision. Fear of not making a decision. Fear of missing God. Fear that God will miss you.

You've asked people what you should do, but they don't know.

Then, in the midst of your panic, you remember that God has never let you down before. He has blessed you by protecting, loving, and being with you through the worst of times.

Why be afraid? Hasn't he already promised you that the latter part of your life will be greater than your past?

Get out of the way and let God be God. He is your Deliverer!

❉

*F*or God hath not given us the spirit of fear; but of power, and of love, and of a sound mind.

2 TIMOTHY 1:7

*H*erein is our love made perfect, that we may have boldness in the day of judgment: because as he is, so are we in this world.

There is not fear in love; but perfect love casteth out fear: because fear hath torment. He that feareth is not made perfect in love.

We love him, because he first loved us.

1 JOHN 4:17–19

*F*or whatsoever is born of God overcometh the world: and this is the victory that overcometh the world, even our faith.

1 JOHN 5:4

*C*asting all your care upon him; for he careth for you.

1 PETER 5:7

Fear not, little flock; for it is your Father's good pleasure to give you the kingdom.

Luke 12:32

Behold, I give unto you power to tread on serpents and scorpions, and over all the power of the enemy: and nothing shall by any means hurt you.

Luke 10:19

These things I have spoken unto you, that in me ye might have peace. In the world ye shall have tribulation: but be of good cheer; I have overcome the world.

John 16:33

Peace I leave with you, my peace I give unto you: not as the world giveth, give I unto you. Let not your heart be troubled, neither let it be afraid.

John 14:27

The grass withereth, the flower fadeth: but the world of our God shall stand for ever.

Isaiah 40:8

But now thus saith the Lord that created thee, O Jacob, and he that formed thee, O Israel, Fear not: for I have redeemed thee, I have called thee by thy name; thou art mine.

When thou passest through the waters, I will be

with thee; and through the rivers, they shall not overflow thee: when thou walkest through the fire, thou shalt not be burned; neither shall the flame kindle upon thee.

ISAIAH 43:1-2

Thou wilt keep him in perfect peace, whose mind is stayed on thee: because he trusteth in thee.

Trust ye in the LORD for ever: for in the LORD JEHOVAH is everlasting strength:

ISAIAH 26:3-4

The angel of the LORD encampeth round about them that fear him, and delivereth them.

PSALMS 34:7

The LORD is my shepherd; I shall not want.

He maketh me to lie down in green pastures: he leadeth me beside the still waters.

He restoreth my soul: he leadeth me in the paths of righteousness for his name's sake.

Yea, though I walk through the valley of the shadow of death, I will fear no evil: for thou art with me; thy rod and thy staff they comfort me.

PSALMS 23:1-4

For he shall give his angels charge over thee, to keep thee in all thy ways.

They shall bear thee up in their hands, lest thou dash thy foot against a stone.

PSALMS 91:11-12

*M*y help cometh from the LORD, which made heaven and earth.

He will not suffer thy foot to be moved: he that keepeth thee will not slumber.

PSALMS 121:2-3

I laid me down and slept; I awaked; for the LORD sustained me.

I will not be afraid of ten thousands of people, that have set themselves against me round about.

PSALMS 3:5-6

*T*hey that sow tears in shall reap in joy.

He that goeth forth and weepeth, bearing precious seed, shall doubtless come again with rejoicing, bringing his sheaves with him.

PSALMS 126:5-6

*M*y soul, wait thou only upon God; for my expectation is from him.

He only is my rock and my salvation: he is my defence; I shall not be moved.

PSALMS 62:5-6

The name of the LORD is a strong tower: the righteous runneth into it, and is safe.

PROVERBS 18:10

Trust in the LORD with all thine heart; and lean not unto thine own understanding.

In all thy ways acknowledge him, and he shall direct thy paths.

PROVERBS 3:5–6

Fear thou not; for I am with thee: be not dismayed; for I am thy God: I will strengthen thee; yea, I will help thee; yea, I will uphold thee with the right hand of my righteousness.

ISAIAH 41:10

But they that wait upon the LORD shall renew their strength; they shall mount up with wings as eagles; they shall run, and not be weary; and they shall walk, and not faint.

ISAIAH 40:31

Therefore I will look unto the Lord; I will wait for the God of my salvation: my God will hear me.

MICAH 7:7

Teaching them to observe all things whatsoever I have commanded you: and, lo, I am with you alway, even unto the end of the world. Amen.

MATTHEW 28:20

Let your conversation be without covetousness; and be content with such things as ye have: for he hath said, I will never leave thee, nor forsake thee.

So that we may boldly say, The Lord is my helper, and I will not fear what man shall do unto me.

HEBREWS 13:5–6

Nay, in all these things we are more than conquerors through him that loved us.

For I am persuaded, that neither death, nor life, nor angels, nor principalities, nor powers, nor things present, nor things to come,

Nor height, nor depth, nor any other creature, shall be able to separate us from the love of God, which is in Christ Jesus our Lord.

ROMANS 8:37–39

What shall we then say to these things? If God be for us, who can be against us?

ROMANS 8:31

And he said unto me, My grace is sufficient for thee: for my strength is made perfect in weakness. Most gladly therefore will I rather glory in my infirmities, that the power of Christ may rest upon me.

2 CORINTHIANS 12:9

Fellowship

It's time spent with God.

HOW OFTEN DO WE THINK about it and say to ourselves, "I'm going to spend some time with the Lord this weekend. Yep, just God and me—listening, talking, and just fellowshipping with my Heavenly Father."

Then comes life. We get busy. We suddenly remember a task we really need to do that we have been putting off for weeks.

That's okay, we tell ourselves. We'll spend time fellowshipping with God right afterwards. But then we need to have a bite to eat before we sit down and begin our consecrated time. Then the telephone rings. A friend is in crisis, and before we know it we are caught up in our day and that precious time we wanted to spend, just us and The Father, has passed.

You're disappointed—mostly in yourself—and even

get into a little condemnation. But, you say to yourself, there is always next week—then you will definitely take the time.

All the while, your Father God waits patiently, never wavering in His commitment to you to tell you the things He wants you to know and to listen to your innermost thoughts. He waits for those still and quiet moments when you have come to Him not even fully aware of your own deepest desires. All because He wants to bless you.

What can be more important than the time you spend with Him?

Come unto me, all ye that labour and are heavy laden, and I will give you rest.

Take my yoke upon you, and learn of me; for I am meek and lowly in heart: and ye shall find rest unto your souls.

For my yoke is easy, and my burden is light.

MATTHEW 11:28-30

This book of the law shall not depart out of thy mouth; but thou shalt meditate therein day and night, that thou mayest observe to do according to all that is written therein: for then thou shalt make thy way prosperous, and then thou shalt have good success.

JOSHUA 1:8

*E*nter into his gates with thanksgiving, and into his courts with praise: be thankful unto him, and bless his name.

For the LORD is good; his mercy is everlasting; and his truth endureth to all generations.

PSALMS 100:4–5

*T*he LORD is nigh unto all them that call upon him, to all that call upon him in truth.

He will fulfil the desire of them that fear him: he also will hear their cry, and will save them.

The LORD preserveth all them that love him: but all the wicked will he destroy.

My mouth shall speak the praise of the LORD: and let all flesh bless his holy name for ever and ever.

PSALMS 145:18–21

*L*ooking unto Jesus the author and finisher of our faith; who for the joy that was set before him endured the cross, despising the shame, and is set down at the right hand of the throne of God.

HEBREWS 12:2

They shall enter into my sanctuary, and they shall come near to my table, to minister unto me, and they shall keep my charge.

EZEKIEL 44:16

For the Lord GOD will help me; therefore shall I not be confounded: therefore have I set my face like a flint, and I know that I shall not be ashamed.

ISAIAH 50:7

The Lord GOD hath opened mine ear, and I was not rebellious, neither turned away back.

ISAIAH 50:5

Thou wilt keep him in perfect peace, whose mind is stayed on thee: because he trusteth in thee.

Trust ye in the LORD for ever: for in the LORD JEHOVAH is everlasting strength:

ISAIAH 26:3-4

It is better to trust in the LORD than to put confidence in man.

PSALMS 118:8

The LORD is my strength and song, and is become my salvation.

PSALMS 118:14

But thou, O Lord, art a shield for me; my glory, and the lifter up of mine head.

Psalms 3:3

My voice shalt thou hear in the morning, O Lord; in the morning will I direct my prayer unto thee, and will look up.

Psalms 5:3

But rather seek ye the kingdom of God; and all these things shall be added unto you.

Luke 12:31

Seek ye the Lord while he may be found, call ye upon him while he is near:

Isaiah 55:6

Yet they seek me daily, and delight to know my ways, as a nation that did righteousness, and forsook not the ordinance of their God: they ask of me the ordinances of justice; they take delight in approaching to God.

Isaiah 58:2

Seek the Lord, and his strength: seek his face evermore.

Remember his marvellous works that he hath done; his wonders, and the judgments of his mouth;

Psalms 105:4–5

But seek ye first the kingdom of God, and his righteousness; and all these things shall be added unto you.

MATTHEW 6:33

And ye shall seek me, and find me, when ye shall search for me with all your heart.

And I will be found of you, saith the LORD: and I will turn away your captivity, and I will gather you from all nations, and from all the places whither I have driven you, saith the LORD; and I will bring you again into the place whence I caused you to be carried away captive.

JEREMIAH 29:13-14

When thou saidst, Seek ye my face; my heart said unto thee, Thy face, LORD, will I seek.

PSALMS 27:8

Let all those that seek thee rejoice and be glad in thee: let such as love thy salvation say continually, The LORD be magnified.

PSALMS 40:16

Ask, and it shall be given you; seek, and ye shall find; knock, and it shall be opened unto you:

MATTHEW 7:7

Finances

He's got you covered.

EVEN BEFORE HE LOST his job, Michael had always been faithful with his finances. He tithed, gave offerings, usually paid cash, and followed a written budget.

He had been laid off for a year, his unemployment benefits had long ago run out, and he had not been able to find full-time work. So he worked where he could, often for a quarter of the money he used to make. And still he tithed and gave offerings.

"I told God that I was going to trust Him and do what He told me to do with my money even if I only had ten cents," Michael said. "I prayed over every paycheck I got and asked God how He wanted me to spend the money before I even went to the bank.

"What I found out was that God had my financial back covered during all that time. Now I look back and I can't figure out how I got through those tough times.

Now I am making pretty good money again but I still go to God with every cent I earn. I learned that it is not how much money you make, but your obedience to God with what you have that counts."

Beloved, I wish above all things that thou mayest prosper and be in health, even as thy soul prospereth.

3 JOHN 2

Honour the LORD with thy substance, and with the firstfruits of all thine increase:

So shall thy barns be filled with plenty, and thy presses shall burst out with new wine.

PROVERBS 3:9–10

I lead in the way of righteousness, in the midst of the paths of judgment:

That I may cause those that love me to inherit substance; and I will fill their treasures.

PROVERBS 8:20–21

And all the tithe of the land, whether of the seed of the land, or of the fruit of the tree, is the LORD'S: it is holy unto the LORD.

LEVITICUS 27:30

But seek ye first the kingdom of God, and his righteousness; and all these things shall be added unto you.

Take therefore no thought for the morrow: for the morrow shall take thought for the things of itself. Sufficient unto the day is the evil thereof.

MATTHEW 6:33-34

*S*aying, Surely blessing I will bless thee, and multiplying I will multiply thee.

And so, after he had patiently endured, he obtained the promise.

HEBREWS 6:14-15

O fear the LORD, ye his saints: for there is no want to them that fear him.

The young lions do lack, and suffer hunger: but they that seek the LORD shall not want any good thing.

PSALMS 34:9-10

*B*lessed is the man that walketh not in the counsel of the ungodly, nor standeth in the way of sinners, nor sitteth in the seat of the scornful.

But his delight is in the law of the LORD; and in his law doth he meditate day and night.

And he shall be like a tree planted by the rivers of

water, that bringeth forth his fruit in his season; his leaf also shall not wither; and whatsoever he doeth shall prosper.

PSALMS 1:1-3

Let them shout for joy, and be glad, that favour my righteous cause: yea, let them say continually, Let the LORD be magnified, which hath pleasure in the prosperity of his servant.

PSALMS 35:27

But thou shalt remember the LORD thy God: for it is he that giveth thee power to get wealth, that he may establish his covenant which he sware unto thy fathers, as it is this day.

DEUTERONOMY 8:18

But this I say, He which soweth sparingly shall reap also sparingly; and he which soweth bountifully shall reap also bountifully.

Every man according as he purposeth in his heart, so let him give; not grudgingly, or of necessity: for God loveth a cheerful giver.

And God is able to make all grace abound toward you; that ye, always having all sufficiency in all things, may abound to every good work:

2 CORINTHIANS 9:6-8

Blessed is he that considereth the poor: the LORD will deliver him in time of trouble.

The LORD will preserve him, and keep him alive; and he shall be blessed upon the earth: and thou wilt not deliver him unto the will of his enemies.

The LORD will strengthen him upon the bed of languishing: thou wilt make all his bed in his sickness.

PSALMS 41:1-3

A little that a righteous man hath is better than the riches of many wicked.

PSALMS 37:16

I have been young, and now am old; yet have I not seen the righteous forsaken, nor his seed begging bread.

PSALMS 37:25

Ye are cursed with a curse: for ye have robbed me, even this whole nation.

Bring ye all the tithes into the storehouse, that there may be meat in mine house, and prove me now herewith, saith the LORD of hosts, if I will not open you the windows of heaven, and pour you out a blessing, that there shall not be room enough to receive it.

And I will rebuke the devourer for your sakes, and he shall not destroy the fruits of your ground; neither shall your vine cast her fruit before the time in the field, saith the LORD of hosts.

And all nations shall call you blessed: for ye shall be a delightsome land, saith the LORD of hosts.

MALACHI 3:9–12

That the blessing of Abraham might come on the Gentiles through Jesus Christ; that we might receive the promise of the Spirit through faith.

GALATIANS 3:14

But my God shall supply all your need according to his riches in glory by Christ Jesus.

PHILIPPIANS 4:19

That ye be not slothful, but followers of them who through faith and patience inherit the promises.

HEBREWS 6:12

Give, and it shall be given unto you; good measure, pressed down, and shaken together, and running over, shall men give into your bosom. For with the same measure that ye mete withal it shall be measured to you again.

LUKE 6:38

Be thou diligent to know the state of thy flocks, and look well to thy herds.

PROVERBS 27:23

He that hath pity upon the poor lendeth unto the LORD; and that which he hath given will he pay him again.

PROVERBS 19:17

Where no counsel is, the people fall: but in the multitude of counselors there is safety.

PROVERBS 11:14

Forgiveness

The choice is not yours!

"SOMETIMES," a wise man said, "people do things to you that there is no way you can forgive them on your own. What you have to do is roll that pain over onto the Lord and forgive, not because you want to, but because you love God more than anything else on this earth and know that He has commanded it."

And when ye stand praying, forgive, if ye have ought against any: that your Father also which is in heaven may forgive you your trespasses.

But if ye do not forgive, neither will your Father which is in heaven forgive your trespasses.

MARK 11:25–26

Verily I say unto you, All sins shall be forgiven unto the sons of men, and blasphemies wherewith soever they shall blaspheme.

MARK 3:28

But I say unto you which hear, Love your enemies, do good to them which hate you,

Bless them that curse you, and pray for them which despitefully use you.

LUKE 6:27–28

Take heed to yourselves: If thy brother trespass against thee, rebuke him; and if he repent, forgive him.

And if he trespass against thee seven times in a day, and seven times in a day turn again to thee, saying, I repent; thou shalt forgive him.

LUKE 17:3–4

Be ye angry, and sin not: let not the sun go down upon your wrath:

Neither give place to the devil.

EPHESIANS 4:26–27

Let all bitterness, and wrath, and anger, and clamour, and evil speaking, be put away from you, with all malice;

And be ye kind one to another, tenderhearted,

forgiving one another, even as God for Christ's sake hath forgiven you.

EPHESIANS 4:31–32

*B*e ye therefore followers of God, as dear children;
    And walk in love, as Christ also hath loved us, and hath given himself for us an offering and a sacrifice to God for a sweetsmelling savour.

EPHESIANS 5:1–2

I, even I, am he that blotteth out thy transgressions for mine own sake, and will not remember thy sins.
    Put me in remembrance: let us plead together: declare thou, that thou mayest be justified.

ISAIAH 43:25–26

*A*nd this is the confidence that we have in him, that, if we ask any thing according to his will, he heareth us:
    And if we know that he hear us, whatsoever we ask, we know that we have the petitions that we desired of him.

1 JOHN 5:14–15

*I*f we confess our sins, he is faithful and just to forgive us our sins, and to cleanse us from all unrighteousness.

1 JOHN 1:9

*F*inally, be ye all of one mind, having compassion one of another, love as brethren, be pitiful, be courteous:

1 PETER 3:8

*L*et him eschew evil, and do good; let him seek peace, and ensue it.

For the eyes of the Lord are over the righteous, and his ears are open unto their prayers: but the face of the Lord is against them that do evil.

1 PETER 3:11-12

*B*ut I say unto you, Love your enemies, bless them that curse you, do good to them that hate you, and pray for them which despitefully use you, and persecute you;

MATTHEW 5:44

*B*ut I say unto you, That ye resist not evil: but whosoever shall smite thee on thy right cheek, turn to him the other also.

MATTHEW 5:39

*T*hen came Peter to him, and said, Lord, how oft shall my brother sin against me, and I forgive him? till seven times?

Jesus said unto him, I say not unto thee, Until seven times: but, Until seventy times seven.

MATTHEW 18:21-22

Great peace have they which love thy law: and nothing shall offend them.

PSALMS 119:165

Commit thy works unto the LORD, and thy thoughts shall be established.

PROVERBS 16:3

If thine enemy be hungry, give him bread to eat; and if he be thirsty, give him water to drink:

For thou shalt heap coals of fire upon his head, and the LORD shall reward thee.

PROVERBS 25:21–22

Rejoice not when thine enemy falleth, and let not thine heart be glad when he stumbleth:

Lest the LORD see it, and it displease him, and he turn away his wrath from him.

PROVERBS 24:17–18

Say not, I will do so to him as he hath done to me: I will render to the man according to his work.

PROVERBS 24:29

Be of the same mind one toward another. Mind not high things, but condescend to men of low estate. Be not wise in your own conceits.

Recompense to no man evil for evil. Provide things honest in the sight of all men.

If it be possible, as much as lieth in you, live peaceably with all men.

ROMANS 12:16–18

*B*e kindly affectioned one to another with brotherly love; in honour preferring one another;

ROMANS 12:10

*A*nd hope maketh not ashamed; because the love of God is shed abroad in our hearts by the Holy Ghost which is given unto us.

ROMANS 5:5

I can do all things through Christ which strengtheneth me.

PHILIPPIANS 4:13

*L*et nothing be done through strife or vainglory; but in lowliness of mind let each esteem other better than themselves.

PHILIPPIANS 2:3

*T*hat ye might walk worthy of the Lord unto all pleasing, being fruitful in every good work, and increasing in the knowledge of God;

COLOSSIANS 1:10

And forgive us our debts, as we forgive our debtors.

MATTHEW 6:12

For if ye forgive men their trespasses, your heavenly Father will also forgive you:

But if ye forgive not men their trespasses, neither will your Father forgive your trespasses.

MATTHEW 6:14–15

Friendships

Be one and you'll have one.

GOOD FRIENDS become all the more important when you are unmarried. But a good friend deserves a good friend.

Take stock of the *relationship* you have with people you call your friends.

Consider new ways to bless your friends. Take the time to tell them how much they mean to you, then work to find small and new ways to bless them.

The better a friend you are, the better a friend you will have.

$\mathcal{H}$e that walketh with wise men shall be wise: but a companion of fools shall be destroyed.

PROVERBS 13:20

*M*ake no friendship with an angry man; and with a furious man thou shalt not go:

Lest thou learn his ways, and get a snare to thy soul.

PROVERBS 22:24–25

A man that hath friends must shew himself friendly: and there is a friend that sticketh closer than a brother.

PROVERBS 18:24

*W*e took sweet counsel together, and walked unto the house of God in company.

PSALMS 55:14

*B*ehold how good and how pleasant it is for brethren to dwell together in unity!

PSALMS 133:1

*B*e ye not unequally yoked together with unbelievers: for what fellowship hath righteousness with unrighteousness? and what communion hath light with darkness?

And what concord hath Christ with Belial? or what part hath he that believeth with an infidel?

And what agreement hath the temple of God with idols? for ye are the temple of the living God; as God hath said, I will dwell in them, and walk in them; and I will be their God, and they shall be my people.

Wherefore come out from among them, and be ye separate, saith the Lord, and touch not the unclean thing; and I will receive you.

And will be a Father unto you, and ye shall be my sons and daughters, saith the Lord Almighty.

2 CORINTHIANS 6:14–18

A froward man soweth strife: and a whisperer separateth chief friends.

PROVERBS 16:28

Let us therefore follow after the things which make for peace, and things wherewith one may edify another.

ROMANS 14:19

Greater love hath no man than this, that a man lay down his life for his friends.

JOHN 15:13

Blessed is the man that walketh not in the counsel of the ungodly, nor standeth in the way of sinners, nor sitteth in the seat of the scornful.

PSALMS 1:1

𝒜 good name is rather to be chosen than great riches, and loving favour rather than silver and gold.

PROVERBS 22:1

𝒯wo are better than one; because they have a good reward for their labour.

For if they fall, the one will lift up his fellow: but woe to him that is alone when he falleth; for he hath not another to help him up.

ECCLESIASTES 4:9-10

𝒥ron sharpeneth iron; so a man sharpeneth the countenance of his friend.

PROVERBS 27:17

Gossip

Who's your mouth on now?

THE BIBLE does not measure "degrees" of sin. Killing someone's reputation is viewed by God as equal to killing them physically.

The next time you decide to pass on or chew on a tidbit, remember what God says about it and ask yourself if it is juicy enough that you are willing to pay the high price for sharing it.

*L*et your speech be always with grace, seasoned with salt, that ye may know how ye ought to answer every man.

COLOSSIANS 4:6

*F*inally, brethren, whatsoever things are true, whatsoever things are honest, whatsoever things are just, whatsoever things are pure, whatsoever things are lovely, whatsoever things are of good report; if there be any virtue, and if there be any praise, think on these things.

PHILIPPIANS 4:8

*L*et no corrupt communication proceed out of your mouth, but that which is good to use of edifying, that it may minister grace unto the hearers.

And grieve not the holy Spirit of God, whereby ye are sealed unto the day of redemption.

Let all bitterness, and wrath, and anger, and clamour, and evil speaking, be put away from you, with all malice.

EPHESIANS 4:29–31

*B*ut foolish and unlearned questions avoid, knowing that they do gender strifes.

2 TIMOTHY 2:23

*F*or God hath not called us unto uncleanness, but unto holiness.

1 THESSALONIANS 4:7

And that ye study to be quiet, and to do your own business, and to work with your own hands, as we commanded you;

That ye may walk honestly toward them that are without, and that ye may have lack of nothing.

1 THESSALONIANS 4:11–12

And as ye would that men should do to you, do ye also to them likewise.

LUKE 6:31

A good man out of the good treasure of his heart bringeth forth that which is good; and an evil man out of the evil treasure of his heart bringeth forth that which is evil: for out of the abundance of the heart his mouth speaketh.

LUKE 6:45

So then they that are in the flesh cannot please God.

ROMANS 8:8

The mouth of the righteous speaketh wisdom, and his tongue talketh of judgment.

The law of his God is in his heart; none of his steps shall slide.

PSALMS 37:30–31

$\mathcal{L}$ORD, who shall abide in thy tabernacle? who shall dwell in thy holy hill?

He that walketh uprightly, and worketh righteousness, and speaketh the truth in his heart.

He that backbiteth not with his tongue, nor doeth evil to his neighbour, nor taketh up a reproach against his neighbour.

PSALMS 15:1–3

$\mathcal{S}$et a watch, O LORD, before my mouth; keep the door of my lips.

PSALMS 141:3

$\mathcal{F}$or he that soweth to his flesh shall of the flesh reap corruption; but he that soweth to the Spirit shall of the Spirit reap life everlasting.

GALATIANS 6:8

$\mathcal{T}$hou are snared with the words of thy mouth, thou art taken with the words of thy mouth.

PROVERBS 6:2

$\mathcal{H}$e that keepeth his mouth keepeth his life: but he that openeth wide his lips shall have destruction.

PROVERBS 13:3

He that despiseth his neighbour sinneth: but he that hath mercy on the poor, happy is he.

PROVERBS 14:21

He that hath no rule over his own spirit is like a city that is broken down, and without walls.

PROVERBS 25:28

We know that we have passed from death unto life, because we love the brethren. He that loveth not his brother abideth in death.

1 JOHN 3:14

And above all things have fervent charity among yourselves: for charity shall cover the multitude of sins.

1 PETER 4:8

For he that will love life, and see good days, let him refrain his tongue from evil, and his lips that they speak no guile:

1 PETER 3:10

Judge not, that ye be not judged.

For with what judgment ye judge, ye shall be judged: and with what measure ye mete, it shall be measured to you again.

MATTHEW 7:1-2

But I say unto you, That every idle word that men shall speak, they shall give account thereof in the day of judgment.

For by thy words thou shalt be justified, and by thy words thou shalt be condemned.

MATTHEW 12:36-37

A new commandment I give unto you, That ye love one another; as I have loved you, that ye also love one another.

By this shall all men know that ye are my disciples, if ye have love one to another.

JOHN 13:34-35

To speak evil of no man, to be no brawlers, but gentle, shewing all meekness unto all men.

TITUS 3:2

If any man among you seem to be religious and bridleth not his tongue, but deceiveth his own heart, this man's religion is vain.

JAMES 1:26

Out of the same mouth proceedeth blessing and cursing. My brethren, these things ought not so to be.

JAMES 3:10

*P*leasant words are as an honeycomb, sweet to the soul, and health to the bones.

PROVERBS 16:24

*T*he words of a talebearer are as wounds, and they go down into the innermost parts of the belly.

PROVERBS 18:8

A man's belly shall be satisfied with the fruit of his mouth; and with the increase of his lips shall he be filled.

Death and life are in the power of the tongue: and they that love it shall eat the fruit thereof.

PROVERBS 18:20–21

*B*e not a witness against thy neighbour without cause; and deceive not with thy lips.

PROVERBS 24:28

Guidance

Let God direct your movements.

THE EASIEST WAY to know if you are going in God's direction is to check yourself. What is your motive for doing what you are doing? Are your actions rooted in The Word of God, or are they rooted in your own lust, covetousness, or pride?

If your way of thinking is not God's way of thinking, then you simply need to change how you think.

J will instruct thee and teach thee in the way which thou shalt go: I will guide thee with mine eye.

PSALMS 32:8

Be of good courage, and he shall strengthen your heart, all ye that hope in the Lord.

PSALMS 31:24

The Lord shall fight for you, and ye shall hold your peace.

EXODUS 14:14

That he would grant you, according to the riches of his glory, to be strengthened with might by his Spirit in the inner man;

EPHESIANS 3:16

And thine ears shall hear a word behind thee, saying, This is the way, walk ye in it, when ye turn to the right hand, and when ye turn to the left.

ISAIAH 30:21

Fear thou not; for I am with thee: be not dismayed; for I am thy God: I will strengthen thee; yea, I will help thee; yea, I will uphold thee with the right hand of my righteousness.

ISAIAH 41:10

Let us therefore come boldly unto the throne of grace, that we may obtain mercy, and find grace to help in time of need.

HEBREWS 4:16

Come, see a man, which told me all things that ever I did: is not this the Christ?

JOHN 4:29

For with God nothing shall be impossible.

LUKE 1:37

A new heart also will I give you, and a new spirit will I put within you: and I will take away the stony heart out of your flesh, and I will give you an heart of flesh.

And I will put my spirit within you, and cause you to walk in my statutes, and ye shall keep my judgments, and do them.

EZEKIEL 36:26–27

Receive my instruction, and not silver; and knowledge rather than choice gold.

PROVERBS 8:10

Counsel is mine, and sound wisdom: I am understanding; I have strength.

PROVERBS 8:14

Thou wilt keep him in perfect peace, whose mind is stayed on thee: because he trusteth in thee.

Trust ye in the Lord for ever: for in the Lord JEHOVAH is everlasting strength:

ISAIAH 26:3–4

For I the Lord thy God will hold thy right hand, saying unto thee, Fear not; I will help thee.

ISAIAH 41:13

I sought the Lord, and he heard me, and delivered me from all my fears.

PSALMS 34:4

Help

He always knows what to do.

CYNTHIA KNEW ALL of her married friends would love to be in her shoes. Oh, they said, how they would like to have a fabulous job already and then have to choose between two *new* fabulous jobs in two *new* fabulous cities.

"Girl," said Girlfriend #1, "think of all the wonderful people you will meet. You will be in such a high-profile position your new theme song will be 'It's Raining Men'!"

"With your new salary you can buy your dream home," said Girlfriend #2. "No sense waiting until you get married to enjoy the best."

But, despite the fact that Cynthia had been waiting for this type of opportunity most of her career, she got a tiny check in her spirit and did not feel the peace of God about either place. One of the things that concerned her was that she had just agreed to set up the new Women's Outreach Ministry at her church. She had not only given her word, but she was also committed to telling others about Christ.

Cynthia decided just to be still and stay where she was. She continued to serve in her church and to work hard on the job that had been a blessing for the last five years.

Six months later, Cynthia's boss, who had always been one of her big supporters, learned of a new position at the company. Although the job required Cynthia to leap several levels above where she currently worked, he believed she could do it and gave her a glowing recommendation.

Cynthia got the job! It was better than either of the other two positions she had been offered, and she could continue to do what she felt was her most important work: telling others about the goodness of God!

*C*all unto me, and I will answer thee, and shew thee great and mighty things, which thou knowest not.

JEREMIAH 33:3

*T*he LORD is nigh unto them that are of a broken heart; and saveth such as be of a contrite spirit.

Many are the afflictions of the righteous: but the LORD delivereth him out of them all.

He keepeth all his bones: not one of them is broken.

Evil shall slay the wicked: and they that hate the righteous shall be desolate.

The LORD redeemeth the soul of his servants: and none of them that trust in him shall be desolate.

PSALMS 34:18–22

He maketh the storm a calm, so that the waves thereof are still.

Then they are glad because they be quiet; so he bringeth them unto their desired haven.

PSALMS 107:29–30

We are troubled on every side, yet not distressed; we are perplexed, but not in despair;

Persecuted, but not forsaken; cast down, but not destroyed;

2 CORINTHIANS 4:8–9

For which cause we faint not; but though our outward man perish, yet the inward man is renewed day by day.

For our light affliction, which is but for a moment, worketh for us a far more exceeding and eternal weight of glory;

While we look not at the things which are seen, but at the things which are not seen: for the things which are seen are temporal; but the things which are not seen are eternal.

2 CORINTHIANS 4:16–18

*A*nd I say unto you, Ask, and it shall be given you; seek, and ye shall find; knock, and it shall be opened unto you.

For every one that asketh receiveth; and he that seeketh findeth; and to him that knocketh it shall be opened.

LUKE 11:9–10

*I*f ye then, being evil, know how to give good gifts unto your children: how much more shall your heavenly Father give the Holy Spirit to them that ask him?

LUKE 11:13

*T*here remaineth therefore a rest to the people of God.

For he that is entered into his rest, he also hath ceased from his own works, as God did from his.

Let us labour therefore to enter into that rest, lest any man fall after the same example of unbelief.

HEBREWS 4:9–11

The LORD is good unto them that wait for him, to the soul that seeketh him.

It is good that a man should both hope and quietly wait for the salvation of the LORD.

LAMENTATIONS 3:25–26

Teach me to do thy will; for thou art my God: thy spirit is good; lead me into the land of uprightness.

Quicken me, O LORD, for thy name's sake: for thy righteousness' sake bring my soul out of trouble.

And of thy mercy cut off mine enemies, and destroy all them that afflict my soul: for I am thy servant.

PSALMS 143:10–12

Our help is in the name of the LORD, who made heaven and earth.

PSALMS 124:8

The LORD is gracious, and full of compassion; slow to anger, and of great mercy.

The LORD is good to all: and his tender mercies are over all his works.

PSALMS 145:8–9

But if the Spirit of him that raised up Jesus from the dead dwell in you, he that raised up Christ from the dead shall also quicken your mortal bodies by his Spirit that dwelleth in you.

ROMANS 8:11

Likewise the Spirit also helpeth our infirmities: for we know not what we should pray for as we ought: but the Spirit itself maketh intercession for us with groaning which cannot be uttered.

And he that searcheth the hearts knoweth what is the mind of the Spirit, because he maketh intercession for the saints according to the will of God.

ROMANS 8:26–27

Then he answered and spake unto me, saying, This is the word of the LORD unto Zerubbabel, saying, Not by might, nor by power, but by my spirit, saith the LORD of hosts.

ZECHARIAH 4:6

Howbeit when he, the Spirit of truth, is come, he will guide you into all truth: for he shall not speak of himself; but whatsoever he shall hear, that shall he speak: and he will shew you things to come.

JOHN 16:13

I will not leave you comfortless: I will come to you.

JOHN 14:18

The blessing of the LORD, it maketh rich, and he addeth no sorrow with it.

PROVERBS 10:22

Jealousy

Why?

THE DEVIL LOVES JEALOUSY because he can use it to open the door to a lot of other stuff in our lives. With jealousy laying the groundwork, he can trick us into being resentful, and confused. He can convince us to gossip (kill someone's reputation with our tongue) and get us involved in strife.

The next time the devil tries to play the jealousy card with you, find a way to bless that person. Then laugh at the devil because once again he has had to learn the hard way that nothing and no one compares to who you are in Christ.

※

*F*or where envying and strife is, there is confusion and every evil work.

JAMES 3:16

*N*ow the works of the flesh are manifest, which are these; Adultery, fornication, uncleanness, lasciviousness,

Idolatry, witchcraft, hatred, variance, emulations, wrath, strife, seditions, heresies,

Envyings, murders, drunkenness, revellings, and such like: of the which I tell you before, as I have also told you in time past, that they which do such things shall not inherit the kingdom of God.

GALATIANS 5:19–21

*F*or, brethren, ye have been called unto liberty; only use not liberty for an occasion to the flesh, but by love serve one another.

For all the law is fulfilled in one word, even in this; Thou shalt love thy neighbour as thyself.

But if ye bite and devour one another, take heed that ye be not consumed one of another.

This I say then, Walk in the Spirit, and ye shall not fulfil the lust of the flesh.

GALATIANS 5:13–16

Let us walk honestly, as in the day; not in rioting and drunkenness, not in chambering and wantonness, not in strife and envying.

But put ye on the Lord Jesus Christ, and make not provision for the flesh, to fulfil the lusts thereof.

ROMANS 13:13–14

He that hath no rule over his own spirit is like a city that is broken down, and without walls.

PROVERBS 25:28

There is a way which seemeth right unto a man, but the end thereof are the ways of death.

PROVERBS 14:12

For jealousy is the rage of a man: therefore he will not spare in the day of vengeance.

PROVERBS 6:34

A naughty person, a wicked man, walketh with a froward mouth.

He winketh with his eyes, he speaketh with his feet, he teacheth with his fingers;

Frowardness is in his heart, he deviseth mischief continually; he soweth discord.

Therefore shall his calamity come suddenly; suddenly shall he be broken without remedy.

These six things doth the LORD hate: yea, seven are an abomination unto him:

A proud look, a lying tongue, and hands that shed innocent blood,

An heart that deviseth wicked imaginations, feet that be swift in running to mischief,

A false witness that speaketh lies, and he that soweth discord among brethren.

PROVERBS 6:12–19

Whoso keepeth his mouth and his tongue keepeth his soul from troubles.

PROVERBS 21:23

Do all things without murmurings and disputings:

That ye may be blameless and harmless, the sons of God, without rebuke, in the midst of a crooked and perverse nation, among whom ye shine as lights in the world;

PHILIPPIANS 2:14–15

But foolish and unlearned questions avoid, knowing that they do gender strifes.

And the servant of the Lord must not strive; but be gentle unto all men, apt to teach, patient,

2 TIMOTHY 23–24

But avoid foolish questions, and genealogies, and contentions, and strivings about the law; for they are unprofitable and vain.

TITUS 3:9

The mouth of the righteous speaketh wisdom, and his tongue talketh of judgment.

The law of his God is in his heart; none of his steps shall slide.

PSALMS 37:30-31

Casting down imaginations, and every high thing that exalted itself against the knowledge of God, and bringing into captivity every thought to the obedience of Christ;

2 CORINTHIANS 10:5

If we live in the Spirit, let us also walk in the Spirit.

Let us not be desirous of vain glory, provoking one another, envying one another.

GALATIANS 5:25-26

Finally, my brethren, be strong in the Lord, and in the power of his might.

EPHESIANS 6:10

Charity suffereth long, and is kind; charity envieth not; charity vaunteth not itself, is not puffed up,

Doth not behave itself unseemly, seeketh not her own, is not easily provoked, thinketh no evil;

Rejoiceth not in iniquity, but rejoiceth in the truth;

1 CORINTHIANS 13:4-6

That the righteousness of the law might be fulfilled in us, who walk not after the flesh, but after the Spirit.

For they that are after the flesh do mind the things of the flesh; but they that are after the Spirit the things of the Spirit.

For to be carnally minded is death; but to be spiritually minded is life and peace.

ROMANS 8:4-6

Strive not with a man without cause, if he have done thee no harm.

Envy thou not the oppressor, and choose none of his ways.

PROVERBS 3:30-31

Go not forth hastily to strive, lest thou know not what to do in the end thereof, when thy neighbour hath put thee to shame.

PROVERBS 25:8

He that passeth by, and meddleth with strife belonging not to him, is like one that taketh a dog by the ears.

PROVERBS 26:17

Let not thine heart envy sinners: but be thou in the fear of the LORD all the day long.

PROVERBS 23:17

Knowing God's Will

If you don't stand for it, you'll fall for anything.

WHEN THE RED LIGHT comes on in our cars, the first thing we do is look in the manual because we know the manufacturer will give us directions on what to do. When we go to a mechanic and the information he gives us does not jibe with the solution given by the manufacturer, we tell the mechanic about it.

When a red light comes on in our lives, we need to go to the manual provided by our manufacturer—the Bible.

In it we will find directions on not only how to fix a problem but also on how everything is supposed to work.

So whenever someone tells us that we have to be sick or broke or unhappy or unmarried, we can tell them that we have read the manual and we choose to believe Our Maker!

Beloved, let us love one another: for love is of God; and every one that loveth is born of God, and knoweth God.

He that loveth not knoweth not God; for God is love.

1 JOHN 4:7–8

Let us therefore come boldly unto the throne of grace, that we may obtain mercy, and find grace to help in time of need.

HEBREWS 4:16

That he would grant you, according to the riches of his glory, to be strengthened with might by his Spirit in the inner man;

That Christ may dwell in your hearts by faith; that ye, being rooted and grounded in love,

May be able to comprehend with all saints what is the breadth, and length, and depth, and height;

And to know the love of Christ, which passeth knowledge, that ye might be filled with all the fullness of God.

Now unto him that is able to do exceeding abundantly above all that we ask or think, according to the power that worketh in us,

EPHESIANS 3:16–20

For therein is the righteousness of God revealed from faith to faith: as it is written. The just shall live by faith.

ROMANS 1:17

For God so loved the world, that he gave his only begotten Son, that whosoever believeth in him should not perish, but have everlasting life.

JOHN 3:16

A new commandment I give unto you, That ye love one another; as I have loved you, that ye also love one another.

By this shall all men know that ye are my disciples, if ye have love one to another.

JOHN 13:34–35

For God hath not given us the spirit of fear; but of power, and of love, and of a sound mind.

2 TIMOTHY 1:7

Thou wilt keep him in perfect peace, whose mind is stayed on thee: because he trusteth in thee.

Trust ye in the Lord for ever: for in the LORD JEHOVAH is everlasting strength:

ISAIAH 26:3–4

Counsel is mine, and sound wisdom: I am understanding; I have strength.

PROVERBS 8:14

I will instruct thee and teach thee in the way which thou shalt go: I will guide thee with mine eye.

PSALMS 32:8

Laziness

Get up and get busy!

IF YOU BELIEVE the God you serve is a "more than enough" God, then why are you willing to accept a "just get by" life?

When we first meet Him in the Bible, God is at work creating the Universe.

Get up and get busy. You don't have to re-create the universe; just put your hands to something that you know how to do and that will move things forward.

God honors work!

$\mathcal{G}$o to the ant, thou sluggard; consider her ways, and be wise:

Which having no guide, overseer, or ruler,

Provideth her meat in the summer, and gathereth her food in the harvest.

How long wilt thou sleep, O sluggard? when wilt thou arise out of thy sleep?

Yet a little sleep, a little slumber, a little folding of the hands to sleep:

So shall thy poverty come as one that travelleth, and thy want as an armed man.

PROVERBS 6:6–11

And let us not be weary in well doing: for in due season we shall reap, if we faint not.

GALATIANS 6:9

That ye be not slothful, but followers of them who through faith and patience inherit the promises.

HEBREWS 6:12

And I will put my spirit within you, and cause you to walk in my statutes, and ye shall keep my judgments, and do them.

EZEKIEL 36:27

Come now, and let us reason together, saith the LORD: though your sins be as scarlet, they shall be as white as snow; though they be red like crimson, they shall be as wool.

If ye be willing and obedient, ye shall eat the good of the land:

ISAIAH 1:18-19

*H*e giveth power to the faint; and to them that have no might he increaseth strength.

Even the youths shall faint and be weary, and the young men shall utterly fall:

But they that wait upon the LORD shall renew their strength; they shall mount up with wings as eagles; they shall run, and not be weary; and they shall walk, and not faint.

ISAIAH 40:29-31

*O*nly be thou strong and very courageous, that thou mayest observe to do according to all the law, which Moses my servant commandeth thee: turn not from it to the right hand or to the left, that thou mayest prosper whithersoever thou goest.

This book of the law shall not depart out of thy mouth; but thou shalt meditate therein day and night, that thou mayest observe to do according to all that is written therein: for then thou shalt make thy way prosperous, and then thou shalt have good success.

JOSHUA 1:7-8

*B*e ye strong therefore, and let not your hands be weak: for your work shall be rewarded.

2 CHRONICLES 15:7

*S*tudy to shew thyself approved unto God, a workman that needeth not to be ashamed, rightly dividing the word of truth.

2 TIMOTHY 2:15

I love them that love me; and those that seek me early shall find me.

PROVERBS 8:17

*L*ove not sleep, lest thou come to poverty; open thine eyes, and thou shalt be satisfied with bread.

PROVERBS 20:13

Loneliness

*Just talk to The One who always wants
to hear from you.*

WHEN WE ARE LONELY, most of us believe it is
because we are unmarried. But that is not so.

Loneliness is *thinking* about being alone *physically,*
then becoming fearful because you *believe* that you are
alone.

Loneliness is a spiritual issue that can be overcome
only by spiritual measures.

God would neither have us lonely nor bring us
loneliness. If you want to kick loneliness out of your
life forever, you must change the way you think. When
we truly believe that God has given us love and is
always there for us, there is no room for talk or feelings
of loneliness and fear.

The next time you find yourself believing that you

are by yourself, have a little chat with Jesus, who has promised never to leave us alone.

The LORD is nigh unto all them that call upon him, to all that call upon him in truth.

He will fulfil the desire of them that fear him: he also will hear their cry, and will save them.

PSALMS 145:18–19

I will lift up mine eyes unto the hills, from whence cometh my help.

My help cometh from the LORD, which made heaven and earth.

He will not suffer thy foot to be moved: he that keepeth thee will not slumber.

PSALMS 121:1–3

But thou, O LORD, art a shield for me; my glory and the lifter up of mine head.

I cried unto the LORD with my voice, and he heard me out of his holy hill. Selah.

PSALMS 3:3–4

I wait for the LORD, my soul doth wait, and in his word do I hope.

PSALMS 130:5

And the peace of God, which passeth all understanding, shall keep your hearts and minds through Christ Jesus.

Finally, brethren, whatsoever things are true, whatsoever things are honest, whatsoever things are just, whatsoever things are pure, whatsoever things are lovely, whatsoever things are of good report; if there be any virtue, and if there be any praise, think on these things.

PHILIPPIANS 4:7–8

Be strong and of a good courage, fear not, nor be afraid of them: for the LORD thy God, he it is that doth go with thee; he will not fail thee, nor forsake thee.

DEUTERONOMY 3:16

Teaching them to observe all things whatsoever I have commanded you: and, lo, I am with you alway, even unto the end of the world. Amen.

MATTHEW 28:20

Behold, the hour cometh, yea, is now come, that ye shall be scattered, every man to his own, and shall leave me alone: and yet I am not alone, because the Father is with me.

These things I have spoken unto you, that in me ye might have peace. In the world ye shall have tribulation: but be of good cheer; I have overcome the world.

JOHN 16:32-33

Casting all your care upon him; for he careth for you.

1 PETER 5:7

Let your conversation be without covetousness; and be content with such things as ye have: for he hath said, I will never leave thee, nor forsake thee.

So that we may boldly say, The Lord is my helper, and I will not fear what man shall do unto me.

HEBREWS 13:5-6

Fear not; for thou shalt be not ashamed: neither be thou confounded; for thou shalt not be put to shame; for thou shalt forget the shame of thy youth, and shalt not remember the reproach of thy widowhood any more.

For thy Maker is thine husband; the LORD of hosts is his name; and thy Redeemer the Holy One of Israel; The God of the whole earth shall he be called.

ISAIAH 54:4-5

Thou wilt keep him in perfect peace, whose mind is stayed on thee: because he trusteth in thee.

Trust ye in the LORD for ever: for in the LORD
JEHOVAH is everlasting strength:

ISAIAH 26:3-4

Who shall separate us from the love of Christ?
shall tribulation, or distress, or persecution, or
famine, or nakedness, or peril, or sword?

As it is written, For thy sake we are killed all the
day long; we are accounted as sheep for the slaughter.

Nay, in all these things we are more than conquerors through him that loved us.

For I am persuaded, that neither death, nor life,
nor angels, nor principalities, nor powers, nor things
present, nor things to come,

Nor height, nor depth, nor any other creature,
shall be able to separate us from the love of God,
which is in Christ Jesus our Lord.

ROMANS 8:35-39

What shall we then say to these things? If God be
for us, who can be against us?

ROMANS 8:31

Fear thou not; for I am with thee: be not dismayed;
for I am thy God: I will strengthen thee; yea, I will
help thee; yea, I will uphold thee with the right hand
of my righteousness.

ISAIAH 41:10

Trust in the Lord with all thine heart; and lean not unto thine own understanding.

In all thy ways acknowledge him, and he shall direct thy paths.

PROVERBS 3:5-6

Why art thou cast down, O my soul? and why art thou disquieted within me? hope in God: for I shall yet praise him, who is the health of my countenance, and my God.

PSALMS 43:5

And they that know thy name will put their trust in thee: for thou, Lord, hast not forsaken them that seek thee.

PSALMS 9:10

Blessed is the man that trusteth in the Lord, and whose hope the Lord is.

For he shall be as a tree planted by the waters, and that spreadeth out her roots by the river, and shall not see when heat cometh, but her leaf shall be green; and shall not be careful in the year of drought, neither shall cease from yielding fruit.

JEREMIAH 17:7-8

And such trust have we through Christ to God-ward:

Not that we are sufficient of ourselves to think any thing as of ourselves; but our sufficiency is of God;

2 CORINTHIANS 3:4–5

*M*y soul, wait thou only upon God; for my expectation is from him.

He only is my rock and my salvation: he is my defence; I shall not be moved.

In God is my salvation and my glory: the rock of my strength, and my refuge, is in God.

Trust in him at all times; ye people, pour out your heart before him: God is a refuge for us. Selah.

PSALMS 62:5–8

*Y*ea, though I walk through the valley of the shadow of death, I will fear no evil: for thou art with me; thy rod and thy staff they comfort me.

PSALMS 23:4

Love

It makes you wanna do right.

SOMETIMES OUR FLESH FIGHTS *so* hard against our spirit. We know the right thing to do but . . .

It's time we stop fighting with our flesh and begin to do the right thing for the *best* reason: because we love God.

When our actions are rooted in love, the punches are taken out of the fight. Love for God takes the "in" out of the "indecision" and pulls the backbone right out from under our stiff necks. Doing the right thing because we love God keeps us from having to worry about whether the other person is worthy of our forgiveness or our kindness, because we already know *He* is.

Let's do right simply because we love The One who loved us first.

Though I speak with the tongues of men and of angels, and have not charity, I am become as sounding brass, or a tinkling cymbal.

And though I have the gift of prophecy, and understand all mysteries, and all knowledge; and though I have all faith, so that I could remove mountains, and have not charity, I am nothing.

And though I bestow all my goods to feed the poor, and though I give my body to be burned, and have not charity, it profiteth me nothing.

Charity suffereth long, and is kind; charity envieth not; charity vaunteth not itself, is not puffed up,

Doth not behave itself unseemly, seeketh not her own, is not easily provoked, thinketh no evil;

Rejoiceth not in iniquity, but rejoiceth in the truth;

Beareth all things, believeth all things, hopeth all things, endureth all things.

Charity never faileth: but whether there be prophecies, they shall fail; whether there be tongues, they shall cease; whether there be knowledge, it shall vanish away.

For we know in part, and we prophesy in part.

But when that which is perfect is come, then that which is in part shall be done away.

When I was a child, I spake as a child, I understood as a child, I thought as a child: but when I became a man, I put away childish things.

For now we see through a glass, darkly; but then face to face: now I know in part; but then shall I know even as also I am known.

And now abideth faith, hope, charity, these three; but the greatest of these is charity.

1 CORINTHIANS 13:1–13

The LORD shall fight for you, and ye shall hold your peace.

EXODUS 14:14

My little children, let us not love in word, neither in tongue; but in deed and in truth.

1 JOHN 3:18

O generation of vipers, how can ye, being evil, speak good things? for out of the abundance of the heart the mouth speaketh.

A good man out of the good treasure of the heart bringeth forth good things: and an evil man out of the evil treasure bringeth forth evil things.

But I say unto you, That every idle word that men shall speak, they shall give account thereof in the day of judgment.

For by thy words thou shalt be justified, and by thy words thou shalt be condemned.

MATTHEW 12:34–37

$\mathcal{Y}$e have heard that it hath been said, Thou shalt love thy neighbour, and hate thine enemy.

But I say unto you, Love your enemies, bless them that curse you, do good to them that hate you, and pray for them which despitefully use you, and persecute you;

That ye may be the children of your Father which is in heaven: for he maketh his sun to rise on the evil and on the good, and sendeth rain on the just and on the unjust.

For if ye love them which love you, what reward have ye? do not even the publicans the same?

And if ye salute your brethren only, what do ye more than others? do not even the publicans so?

Be ye therefore perfect, even as your Father which is in heaven is perfect.

MATTHEW 5:43–48

$\mathcal{F}$or if ye love them which love you, what thank have ye? for sinners also love those that love them.

And if ye do good to them which do good to you, what thank have ye? for sinners also do even the same.

And if ye lend to them of whom ye hope to receive, what thank have ye? for sinners also lend to sinners, to receive as much again.

But love ye your enemies, and do good, and lend, hoping for nothing again; and your reward shall be great, and ye shall be the children of the Highest: for he is kind unto the unthankful and to the evil.

LUKE 6:32–35

This is my commandment, That ye love one another, as I have loved you. Greater love hath no man than this, that a man lay down his life for his friends.

JOHN 15:12–13

Loving the One You Are With

*Run, run, run . . . this is not where
you want to be.*

SOMETIMES THE SIMPLE TRUTH is that they just
look good to us. We are attracted to them, and it is
clear they feel the same about us.

There is only one problem. Not only do they not
know Jesus, we already know that we might just forget
about Him ourselves if we keep hanging out!

Run. Run. Run in the other direction.

God wants only the best for us, and He would never
send anyone who would stand in the way of our relationship with Him.

There is nothing and no one important enough to
disrupt our personal relationship with Christ.

Wake up! No matter how good others look, there is none like Him.

Giving thanks unto the Father, which hath made us meet to be partakers of the inheritance of the saints in light:

Who hath delivered us from the power of darkness, and hath translated us into the kingdom of his dear Son:

In whom we have redemption through his blood, even the forgiveness of sins:

COLOSSIANS 1:12–14

Finally, my brethren, be strong in the Lord, and in the power of his might.

EPHESIANS 6:10

And grieve not the holy Spirit of God, whereby ye are sealed unto the day of redemption.

EPHESIANS 4:30

Fear thou not; for I am with thee: be not dismayed; for I am thy God: I will strengthen thee; yea, I will help thee; yea, I will uphold thee with the right hand of my righteousness.

ISAIAH 41:10

*T*hy word have I hid in mine heart, that I might not sin against thee.

PSALMS 119:11

*B*ut thou, O LORD, art a shield for me; my glory, and the lifter up of mine head.

PSALMS 3:3

*F*or he that soweth to his flesh shall of the flesh reap corruption; but he that soweth to the Spirit shall of the Spirit reap life everlasting.

GALATIANS 6:8

*T*he Lord knoweth how to deliver the godly out of temptations, and to reserve the unjust unto the day of judgment to be punished:

2 PETER 2:9

(*F*or the weapons of our warfare are not carnal, but mighty through God to the pulling down of strong holds;)

Casting down imaginations, and every high thing that exalted itself against the knowledge of God, and bringing into captivity every thought to the obedience of Christ;

2 CORINTHIANS 10:4-5

*F*or we must all appear before the judgment seat of Christ; that every one may receive the things done in his body, according to that he hath done, whether it be good or bad.

2 CORINTHIANS 5:10

*F*or nothing is secret, that shall not be made manifest; neither any thing hid, that shall not be known and come abroad.

LUKE 8:17

*F*or there is nothing covered, that shall not be revealed; neither hid, that shall not be known.

Therefore whatsoever ye have spoken in darkness shall be heard in the light; and that which ye have spoken in the ear in closets shall be proclaimed upon the housetops.

LUKE 12:2-3

*C*an a man take fire in his bosom, and his clothes not be burned?

Can one go upon hot coals, and his feet not be burned?

So he that goeth in to his neighbour's wife; whosoever toucheth her shall not be innocent. . . .

But whoso committeth adultery with a woman lacketh understanding: he that doeth it destroyeth his own soul.

PROVERBS 6:27-29, 32

For the LORD shall be thy confidence, and shall keep thy foot from being taken.

PROVERBS 3:26

He that covereth his sins shall not prosper; but whoso confesseth and forsaketh them shall have mercy.

PROVERBS 28:13

For all that is in the world, the lust of the flesh, and the lust of the eyes, and the pride of life, is not of the Father, but is of the world.

1 JOHN 2:16

We know that whosoever is born of God sinneth not; but he that is begotten of God keepeth himself, and that wicked one toucheth him not.

1 JOHN 5:18

For this is the will of God, even your sanctification, that ye should abstain from fornication:

That every one of you should know how to possess his vessel in sanctification and honour;

Not in the lust of concupiscence, even as the Gentiles which know not God:

That no man go beyond and defraud his brother in any matter: because that the Lord is the avenger of all such, as we also have forewarned you and testified.

For God hath not called us unto uncleanness, but unto holiness.

1 Thessalonians 4:3–7

*A*bstain from all appearance of evil.

And the very God of peace sanctify you wholly; and I pray God your whole spirit and soul and body be preserved blameless unto the coming of our Lord Jesus Christ.

1 Thessalonians 5:22–23

*S*ubmit yourselves therefore to God. Resist the devil, and he will flee from you.

James 4:7

*B*lessed is the man that endureth temptation: for when he is tried, he shall receive the crown of life, which the Lord hath promised to them that love him.

Let no man say when he is tempted, I am tempted of God: for God cannot be tempted with evil, neither tempteth he any man:

But every man is tempted, when he is drawn away of his own lust, and enticed.

Then when lust hath conceived, it bringeth forth sin: and sin, when it is finished, bringeth forth death.

Do not err, my beloved brethren.

James 1:12–16

$\mathcal{I}$ beseech you therefore, brethren, by the mercies of God, that ye present your bodies a living sacrifice, holy, acceptable unto God, which is your reasonable service.

ROMANS 12:1

$\mathcal{A}$nd be not conformed to this world: but be ye transformed by the renewing of your mind, that ye may prove what is that good, and acceptable, and perfect, will of God.

ROMANS 12:2

$\mathcal{F}$or the wrath of God is revealed from heaven against all ungodliness and unrighteousness of men, who hold the truth in unrighteousness;

ROMANS 1:18

$\mathcal{S}$o then they that are in the flesh cannot please God.

ROMANS 8:8

$\mathcal{A}$nd he said, That which cometh out of the man, that defileth the man.

For from within, out of the heart of men, proceed evil thoughts, adulteries, fornications, murders,

Thefts, covetousness, wickedness, deceit, lasciviousness, an evil eye, blasphemy, pride, foolishness:

All these evil things come from within, and defile the man.

MARK 7:20–23

*Y*e have heard that it was said by them of old time, Thou shalt not commit adultery:

But I say unto you, That whosoever looketh on a woman to lust after her hath committed adultery with her already in his heart.

MATTHEW 5:27–28

*A*nd lead us not into temptation, but deliver us from evil: For thine is the kingdom, and the power, and the glory, for ever. Amen.

MATTHEW 6:13

*W*atch and pray, that ye enter not into temptation: the spirit indeed is willing, but the flesh is weak.

MATTHEW 26:41

Ministry

You're called—what now?

EVERYONE SAYS YOU HAVE a call from God on your life. Even more importantly, *you* know it. Although you are unmarried now, you really want to be married one day.

There are a lot of men who don't want their wives to be distracted from the home by demands of the ministry. There are a lot of women who cringe at the thought of being the First Lady of a church.

Those are the ones you should *not* marry.

God will drop the vision He has for our life into the heart of the man or woman He has for us. The right one will be as dedicated to that vision and as passionate about it as you.

Our first step? Do what God tells us to do and let Him run the romance department in our lives.

✳

Study to shew thyself approved unto God, a workman that needeth not to be ashamed, rightly dividing the word of truth.

2 TIMOTHY 2:15

And the servant of the Lord must not strive; but be gentle unto all men, apt to teach, patient,

In meekness instructing those that oppose themselves; if God peradventure will give them repentance to the acknowledging of the truth;

2 TIMOTHY 2:24–25

All scripture is given by inspiration of God, and is profitable for doctrine, for reproof, for correction, for instruction in righteousness:

That the man of God may be perfect, thoroughly furnished unto all good works.

2 TIMOTHY 3:16–17

Now therefore go, and I will be with thy mouth, and teach thee what thou shalt say.

EXODUS 4:12

This book of the law shall not depart out of thy mouth; but thou shalt meditate therein day and night, that thou mayest observe to do according to all that is written therein: for then thou shalt make thy way prosperous, and then thou shalt have good success.

JOSHUA 1:8

And let us not be weary in well doing: for in due season we shall reap, if we faint not.

GALATIANS 6:9

Trust in him at all times: ye people, pour out your heart before him: God is a refuge for us. Selah.

PSALMS 62:8

Blessed is the man that walketh not in the counsel of the ungodly, nor standeth in the way of sinners, nor sitteth in the seat of the scornful.

But his delight is in the law of the LORD; and in his law doth he meditate day and night.

And he shall be like a tree planted by the rivers of water, that bringeth forth his fruit in his season; his leaf also shall not wither; and whatsoever he doeth shall prosper.

PSALMS 1:1–3

Counsel is mine, and sound wisdom: I am understanding; I have strength.

PROVERBS 8:14

*P*ride goeth before destruction, and an haughty spirit before a fall.

Better it is to be of an humble spirit with the lowly, than to divide the spoil with the proud.

PROVERBS 16:18-19

*T*rust in the LORD with all thine heart; and lean not unto thine own understanding.

In all thy ways acknowledge him, and he shall direct thy paths.

Be not wise in thine own eyes: fear the LORD, and depart from evil.

PROVERBS 3:5-7

*M*y son, attend to my words; incline thine ear unto my sayings.

Let them not depart from thine eyes; keep them in the midst of thine heart.

For they are life unto those that find them, and health to all their flesh.

Keep thy heart with all diligence; for out of it are the issues of life.

Put away from thee a froward mouth, and perverse lips put far from thee.

PROVERBS 4:20-24

*B*etter is the poor that walketh in his integrity, than he that is perverse in his lips, and is a fool.

PROVERBS 19:1

*A*nd wisdom and knowledge shall be the stability of thy times, and strength of salvation: the fear of the LORD is his treasure.

ISAIAH 33:6

*T*hou wilt keep him in perfect peace, whose mind is stayed on thee: because he trusteth in thee.

Trust ye in the LORD for ever: for in the LORD JEHOVAH is everlasting strength:

ISAIAH 26:3-4

*T*he Spirit of the Lord GOD is upon me; because the LORD hath anointed me to preach good tidings unto the meek; he hath sent me to bind up the broken-hearted, to proclaim liberty to the captives, and the opening of the prison to them that are bound;

To proclaim the acceptable year of the LORD, and the day of vengeance of our God; to comfort all that mourn;

To appoint unto them that mourn in Zion, to give unto them beauty for ashes, the oil of joy for mourning, the garment of praise for the spirit of heaviness; that they might be called trees of righteousness, the planting of the LORD, that might be glorified.

ISAIAH 61:1–3

*A*nd thine ears shall hear a word behind thee, saying, This is the way, walk ye in it, when ye turn to the right hand, and when ye turn to the left.

ISAIAH 30:21

*M*y people are destroyed for lack of knowledge: because thou hast rejected knowledge, I will also reject thee, that thou shalt be no priest to me: seeing thou hast forgotten the law of thy God, I will also forget thy children.

HOSEA 4:6

*A*nd ye shall seek me, and find me, when ye shall search for me with all your heart.

JEREMIAH 29:13

*B*e not afraid of their faces: for I am with thee to deliver thee, saith the LORD.

JEREMIAH 1:8

*H*umble yourselves in the sight of the Lord, and he shall lift you up.

JAMES 4:10

The integrity of the upright shall guide them: but the perverseness of transgressors shall destroy them.

PROVERBS 11:3

A good name is rather to be chosen than great riches, and loving favour rather than silver and gold.

PROVERBS 22:1

The spirit of a man will sustain his infirmity; but a wounded spirit who can bear?

PROVERBS 18:14

Overcoming Mess

You can't do it by yourself.

A LOT OF THE TIME it takes boldness to overcome mess. Boldness to stand with no *visible* backup. Boldness to stand up for what is right. And boldness to have the determination to claim what God wants to manifest in your life.

Jesus walked on the earth with boldness because He *knew* what His purpose was, and He was determined to do His Father's will even unto death.

Well, Praise God, we can have the same attitude!

We are to pray to God for the boldness we need to do whatever is necessary to get past the mess in our life and get the job He has placed before each of us done.

The LORD lift up his countenance upon thee, and give thee peace.

NUMBERS 6:26

Herein is our love made perfect, that we may have boldness in the day of judgment: because as he is, so are we in this world.

There is no fear in love; but perfect love casteth out fear: because fear hath torment. He that feareth is not made perfect in love.

We love him, because he first loved us.

1 JOHN 4:17–19

For the LORD shall be thy confidence, and shall keep thy foot from being taken.

PROVERBS 3:26

The name of the LORD is a strong tower: the righteous runneth into it, and is safe.

PROVERBS 18:10

Let this mind be in you, which was also in Christ Jesus:

PHILIPPIANS 2:5

And the peace of God, which passeth all understanding, shall keep your hearts and minds through Christ Jesus.

Finally, brethren, whatsoever things are true, whatsoever things are honest, whatsoever things are just, whatsoever things are pure, whatsoever things are lovely, whatsoever things are of good report; if there be any virtue, and if there be any praise, think on these things.

PHILIPPIANS 4:7–8

Wait on the LORD: be of good courage, and he shall strengthen thine heart: wait, I say, on the LORD.

PSALMS 27:14

I will bless the LORD, who hath given me counsel: my reins also instruct me in the night seasons.

I have set the LORD always before me: because he is at my right hand, I shall not be moved.

Therefore my heart is glad, and my glory rejoiceth: my flesh also shall rest in hope.

PSALMS 16:7–9

Seek the LORD and his strength, seek his face continually.

Remember his marvellous works that he hath done, his wonders, and the judgments of his mouth;

1 CHRONICLES 16:11–12

Casting all your care upon him; for he careth for you.

1 PETER 5:7

Let us therefore follow after the things which make for peace, and things wherewith one may edify another.

ROMANS 14:19

And the cares of this world, and the deceitfulness of riches, and the lusts of other things entering in, choke the word, and it becometh unfruitful.

MARK 4:19

Wherefore seeing we also are compassed about with so great a cloud of witnesses, let us lay aside every weight, and the sin which doth so easily beset us, and let us run with patience the race that is set before us,

HEBREWS 12:1

Peace I leave with you, my peace I give unto you: not as the world giveth, give I unto you. Let not your heart be troubled, neither let it be afraid.

JOHN 14:27

For with God nothing shall be impossible.

LUKE 1:37

And take heed to yourselves, lest at any time your hearts be overcharged with surfeiting, and drunkenness, and cares of this life, and so that day come upon you unawares.

LUKE 21:34

*F*inally, my brethren, be strong in the Lord, and in the power of his might.

EPHESIANS 6:10

*W*herefore take unto you the whole armour of God, that ye may be able to withstand in the evil day, and having done all, to stand.

EPHESIANS 6:13

*F*or who hath known the mind of the Lord, that he may instruct him? But we have the mind of Christ.

1 CORINTHIANS 2:16

*F*ear thou not; for I am with thee: be not dismayed; for I am thy God: I will strengthen thee; yea, I will help thee; yea, I will uphold thee with the right hand of my righteousness.

ISAIAH 41:10

*C*all unto me, and I will answer thee, and shew thee great and mighty things, which thou knowest not.

JEREMIAH 33:3

Patience

You've got to have it.

THERE ARE FEW THINGS that are fun to wait for.

Imagine how God feels waiting for us to get *Him*. Still, He waits patiently while we try out a variety of theories about Him and a boatload of ways to get around doing it *exactly* as He told us to.

Still He waits.

Wouldn't it be nice if we could show just a little bit of that patience with one another? Maybe not be in such a hurry when we find ourselves driving behind someone who isn't quite sure where that right turn should be made. Or how about settling down peacefully behind the person who has just unloaded fifty items onto the checkout belt at the grocery in the fifteen-items-or-less line?

Patience, we are told, is a virtue, a good quality.

When we slow down we put ourselves in one place long enough to be blessed, and all things are possible!

✳

*F*or ye have need of patience, that, after ye have done the will of God, ye might receive the promise.

HEBREWS 10:36

*M*y brethren, count it all joy when ye fall into divers temptations;

Knowing this, that the trying of your faith worketh patience.

But let patience have her perfect work, that ye may be perfect and entire, wanting nothing.

JAMES 1:2–4

*W*hereby are given unto us exceeding great and precious promises: that by these ye might be partakers of the divine nature, having escaped the corruption that is in the world through lust.

And beside this, giving all diligence, add to your faith virtue; and to virtue knowledge;

And to knowledge temperance; and to temperance patience; and to patience godliness;

And to godliness brotherly kindness; and to brotherly kindness charity.

For if these things be in you, and abound, they make you that ye shall neither be barren nor unfruitful in the knowledge of our Lord Jesus Christ.

But he that lacketh these things is blind, and cannot see afar off, and hath forgotten that he was purged from his old sins.

2 PETER 1:4–9

Strengthen with all might, according to his glorious power, unto all patience and longsuffering with joyfulness;

COLOSSIANS 1:11

With all lowliness and meekness, with longsuffering, forbearing one another in love;

EPHESIANS 4:2

That ye be not slothful, but followers of them who through faith and patience inherit the promises.

HEBREWS 6:12

And so, after he had patiently endured, he obtained the promise.

HEBREWS 6:15

And not only so, but we glory in tribulations also: knowing that tribulation worketh patience;

And patience, experience; and experience, hope:

And hope maketh not ashamed; because the love of God is shed abroad in our hearts by the Holy Ghost which is given unto us.

ROMANS 5:3–5

But thou, O man of God, flee these things; and follow after righteousness, godliness, faith, love, patience, meekness.

Fight the good fight of faith, lay hold on eternal life, whereunto thou are also called, and hast professed a good profession before many witnesses.

1 TIMOTHY 6:11–12

Now we exhort you, brethren, warn them that are unruly, comfort the feebleminded, support the weak, be patient toward all men.

1 THESSALONIANS 5:14

For whatsoever things were written aforetime were written for our learning, that we through patience and comfort of the scriptures might have hope.

ROMANS 15:4

$\mathcal{R}$est in the Lord, and wait patiently for him: fret not thyself because of him who prospereth in his way, because of the man who bringeth devices to pass.

Cease from anger, and forsake wrath: fret not thyself in any wise to do evil.

For evildoers shall be cut off: but those that wait upon the Lord, they shall inherit the earth.

PSALMS 37:7–9

$\mathcal{B}$etter is the end of a thing than the beginning thereof: and the patient in spirit is better than the proud in spirit.

Be not hasty in thy spirit to be angry: for anger resteth in the bosom of fools.

ECCLESIASTES 7:8–9

Peace

It's a God thang!

IT SHOULD NOT MATTER what is going on around us. It should not matter what is being said to us or about us. There is a place deep inside each believer in which only the Spirit of God dwells. It is a place to which we can retreat when it all gets to be too much.

If we have trouble finding our way to this place, it is because we are dragging our concerns and troubles there with us. There's no room!

Only you, God, and His perfect peace are allowed.

*P*eace I leave with you, my peace I give unto you: not as the world giveth, give I unto you. Let not your heart be troubled, neither let it be afraid.

JOHN 14:27

Thou wilt keep him in perfect peace, whose mind is stayed on thee: because he trusteth in thee.

Trust ye in the Lord for ever: for the Lord Jehovah is everlasting strength:

ISAIAH 26:3–4

And whatsoever we ask, we receive of him, because we keep his commandments, and do those things that are pleasing in his sight.

1 JOHN 3:22

And let the peace of God rule in your hearts, to the which also ye are called in one body; and be ye thankful.

COLOSSIANS 3:15

Therefore being justified by faith, we have peace with God through our Lord Jesus Christ:

ROMANS 5:1

For to be carnally minded is death; but to be spiritually minded is life and peace.

ROMANS 8:6

And let us not be weary in well doing: for in due season we shall reap, if we faint not.

GALATIANS 6:9

But the fruit of the Spirit is love, joy, peace, long-suffering, gentleness, goodness, faith,

GALATIANS 5:22

I will both lay me down in peace, and sleep: for thou, LORD, only makest me dwell in safety.

PSALMS 4:8

Rest in the LORD, and wait patiently for him: fret not thyself because of him who prospereth in his way, because of the man who bringeth wicked devices to pass.

PSALMS 37:7

Now the Lord of peace himself give you peace always by all means. The Lord be with you all.

2 THESSALONIANS 3:16

And the Lord shall deliver me from every evil work, and will preserve me unto his heavenly kingdom: to whom be glory for ever and ever. Amen.

2 TIMOTHY 4:18

Follow peace with all men, and holiness, without which no man shall see the Lord.

HEBREWS 12:14

*B*ut the wisdom that is from above is first pure, then peaceable, gentle, and easy to be intreated, full of mercy and good fruits, without partiality, and without hypocrisy.

And the fruit of righteousness is sown in peace of them that make peace.

JAMES 3:17–18

*F*inally, brethren, farewell. Be perfect, be of good comfort, be of one mind, live in peace; and the God of love and peace shall be with you.

2 CORINTHIANS 13:11

*B*e careful for nothing; but in every thing by prayer and supplication with thanksgiving let your requests be made known unto God.

And the peace of God, which passeth all understanding, shall keep your hearts and minds through Christ Jesus.

Finally, brethren, whatsoever things are true, whatsoever things are honest, whatsoever things are just, whatsoever things are pure, whatsoever things are lovely, whatsoever things are of good report; if there be any virtue, and if there be any praise, think on these things.

PHILIPPIANS 4:6–8

These things I have spoken unto you, that in me ye might have peace. In the world ye shall have tribulation: but be of good cheer; I have overcome the world.

JOHN 16:33

The LORD will give strength unto his people; the LORD will bless his people with peace.

PSALMS 29:11

Praise

It makes you want to shout!

As unmarrieds we should out-praise anyone.

We have the time because we have the solitude to freely—without a bit of self-conscious restraint—dance, jump, magnify and rave about the goodness of God at the top of our lungs (He likes His praise loud).

He is an awesome, faithful, and worthy God! Shout to the Lord!

I will love thee, O LORD, my strength.

The LORD is my rock, and my fortress, and my deliverer; my God, my strength, in whom I will trust; my buckler, and the horn of my salvation, and my high tower.

I will call upon the LORD, who is worthy to be praised: so shall I be saved from mine enemies.

PSALMS 18:1–3

Our help is in the name of the LORD, who made heaven and earth.

PSALMS 124:8

Make a joyful noise unto the LORD, all ye lands.

Serve the LORD with gladness: come before his presence with singing.

Know ye that the LORD he is God: it is he that hath made us, and not we ourselves; we are his people, and the sheep of his pasture.

Enter into his gates with thanksgiving, and into his courts with praise: be thankful unto him, and bless his name.

For the LORD is good; his mercy is everlasting; and his truth endureth to all generations.

PSALMS 100:1–5

In every thing give thanks: for this is the will of God in Christ Jesus concerning you.

1 THESSALONIANS 5:18

Rejoice in the Lord always: and again I say, Rejoice.

PHILIPPIANS 4:4

Give unto the LORD the glory due unto his name: bring an offering, and come before him: worship the LORD in the beauty of holiness.

1 CHRONICLES 16:29

Let the heaven be glad, and let the earth rejoice: and let men say among the nations, The LORD reigneth.

1 CHRONICLES 16:31

By him therefore let us offer the sacrifice of praise to God continually, that is, the fruit of our lips giving thanks to his name.

HEBREWS 13:15

Praise ye the LORD. Praise God in his sanctuary: praise him in the firmament of his power.

Praise him for his mighty acts: praise him according to his excellent greatness.

Praise him with the sound of the trumpet: praise him with the psaltery and harp.

Praise him with the timbrel and dance: praise him with stringed instruments and organs.

Praise him upon the loud cymbals: praise him upon the high sounding cymbals.

Let every thing that hath breath praise the LORD. Praise ye the LORD.

PSALMS 150

Sing praises to the LORD, which dwelleth in Zion: declare among the people his doings.

PSALMS 9:11

My mouth shall speak the praise of the LORD: and let all flesh bless his holy name for ever and ever.

PSALMS 145:21

Praise ye the LORD. Praise the LORD, O my soul.

While I live will I praise the LORD: I will sing praises unto my God while I have any being.

PSALMS 146:1-2

Preparing for My Husband

It's a Boaz thing. Your girlfriends may not understand.

YOLANDA MET a very nice man at the grocery store. She asked a few pointed and quick questions and found out he was unmarried, heterosexual, and loved God. They began to talk on the telephone a lot and were amazed at how much they had in common.

Before their first date Yolanda had told her girlfriends about him but did not invite him to meet them for about six months.

After they finally did meet, her telephone was ringing when she walked in the door. Her girlfriends were both on the other end. "Yolanda, he's ugly," they said. "Out of all the men in the world and out of all the men you've dated, why would you be interested in *him*?"

"I'm not looking for all the men in the world." Yolanda laughed. "I have been living holy and waiting for God to send me my Boaz—someone who thinks of me before he thinks of himself, someone who is ready to step up to the plate and be the head of a godly household, and someone who loves and serves the same God as me. As far as I can tell, so far he is what I have been praying for. And he looks good to *me*!"

As unmarried Christian women, we need to begin basing our decision about a mate on God's standards—not on those of society, of our family, or of our girlfriends. When we do, we release the power of God into the relationship, and it will be blessed!

❈

Who can find a virtuous woman? for her price is far above rubies.

The heart of her husband doth safely trust in her, so that he shall have no need of spoil.

She will do him good and not evil all the days of her life.

She seeketh wool, and flax, and worketh willingly with her hands.

She is like the merchant's ships; she bringeth her food from afar.

She riseth also while it is yet night, and giveth meat to her household, and a portion to her maidens.

She considereth a field, and buyeth it: with the fruit of her hands she planteth a vineyard.

She girdeth her loins with strength, and strengtheneth her arms.

She perceiveth that her merchandise is good: her candle goeth not out by night.

She layeth her hands to the spindle, and her hands hold the distaff.

She stretcheth out her hand to the poor; yea, she reacheth forth her hands to the needy.

She is not afraid of the snow for her household: for all her household are clothed with scarlet.

She maketh herself coverings of tapestry; her clothing is silk and purple.

Her husband is known in the gates, when he sitteth among the elders of the land.

She maketh fine linen, and selleth it; and delivereth girdles unto the merchant.

Strength and honour are her clothing; and she shall rejoice in time to come.

She openeth her mouth with wisdom; and in her tongue is the law of kindness.

She looketh well to the ways of her household, and eateth not the bread of idleness.

Her children arise up, and call her blessed; her husband also, and he praiseth her.

Many daughters have done virtuously, but thou excellest them all.

Favour is deceitful, and beauty is vain: but a woman that feareth the LORD, she shall be praised.

Give her of the fruit of her hands; and let her own works praise her in the gates.

PROVERBS 31:10-31

Be ye not unequally yoked together with unbelievers: for what fellowship hath righteousness with unrighteousness? and what communion hath light with darkness?

And what concord hath Christ with Belial? or what part hath he that believeth with an infidel?

And what agreement hath the temple of God with idols? for ye are the temple of the living God; as God hath said, I will dwell in them, and walk in them; and I will be their God, and they shall be my people.

Wherefore come out from among them, and be ye separate, saith the Lord, and touch not the unclean thing; and I will receive you,

And will be a Father unto you, and ye shall be my sons and daughters, saith the Lord Almighty.

2 CORINTHIANS 6:14-18

And this is the confidence that we have in him, that, if we ask any thing according to his will, he heareth us:

And if we know that he hear us, whatsoever we ask,

we know that we have the petitions that we desired of him.

1 JOHN 5:14–15

$\mathcal{B}$e careful for nothing; but in every thing by prayer and supplication with thanksgiving let your requests be made known unto God.

And the peace of God, which passeth all understanding, shall keep your hearts and minds through Christ Jesus.

PHILIPPIANS 4:6–7

$\mathcal{N}$evertheless let every one of you in particular so love his wife even as himself; and the wife see that she reverence her husband.

EPHESIANS 5:33

$\mathcal{T}$herefore shall a man leave his father and his mother, and shall cleave unto his wife: and they shall be one flesh.

And they were both naked, the man and his wife, and were not ashamed.

GENESIS 2:24–25

$\mathcal{A}$nd ye are complete in him, which is the head of all principality and power:

COLOSSIANS 2:10

Delight thyself also in the LORD; and he shall give thee the desires of thine heart.

Commit thy way unto the LORD; trust also in him; and he shall bring it to pass.

PSALMS 37:4-5

Rest in the LORD, and wait patiently for him: fret not thyself because of him who prospereth in his way, because of the man who bringeth wicked devices to pass.

PSALMS 37:7

The integrity of the upright shall guide them: but the perverseness of transgressors shall destroy them.

PROVERBS 11:3

To every thing there is a season, and a time to every purpose under the heaven:

ECCLESIASTES 3:1

He hath made every thing beautiful in his time: also he hath set the world in their heart, so that no man can find out the work that God maketh from the beginning to the end.

ECCLESIASTES 3:11

*F*or with God nothing shall be impossible.

LUKE 1:37

*L*et us hold fast the profession of our faith without wavering; (for he is faithful that promised;)

HEBREWS 10:23

*B*ut seek ye first the kingdom of God, and his righteousness; and all these things shall be added unto you.

MATTHEW 6:33

*Y*e are the light of the world. A city that is set on an hill cannot be hid.

MATTHEW 5:14

*B*ut I would have you without carefulness. He that is unmarried careth for the things that belong to the Lord, how he may please the Lord:

1 CORINTHIANS 7:32

*T*here is difference also between a wife and a virgin. The unmarried woman careth for the things of the Lord, that she may be holy both in body and in spirit: but she that is married careth for the things of the world, how she may please her husband.

1 CORINTHIANS 7:34

*I*f ye abide in me, and my words abide in you, ye shall ask what ye will, and it shall be done unto you.

JOHN 15:7

*W*ait on the LORD: be of good courage, and he shall strengthen thine heart: wait, I say, on the LORD.

PSALMS 27:14

*M*y soul, wait thou only upon God; for my expectation is from him.

PSALMS 62:5

*E*very wise woman buildeth her house: but the foolish plucketh it down with her hands.

PROVERBS 14:1

*B*ut my God shall supply all your need according to his riches in glory by Christ Jesus.

PHILIPPIANS 4:19

*L*et your speech be alway with grace, seasoned with salt, that ye may know how ye ought to answer every man.

COLOSSIANS 4:6

But I would have you know, that the head of every man is Christ; and the head of the woman is the man; and the head of Christ is God.

1 CORINTHIANS 11:3

And let us not be weary in well doing: for in due season we shall reap, if we faint not.

GALATIANS 6:9

And the LORD shall guide thee continually, and satisfy thy soul in drought, and make fat thy bones: and thou shalt be like a watered garden, and like a spring of water, whose waters fail not.

ISAIAH 58:11

Cast not away therefore your confidence, which hath great recompense of reward.

For ye have need of patience, that, after ye have done the will of God, ye might receive the promise.

HEBREWS 10:35-35

But they that wait upon the LORD shall renew their strength; they shall mount up with wings as eagles; they shall run, and not be weary; and they shall walk, and not faint.

ISAIAH 40:31

Preparing for My Wife

I can feel my helpmeet coming on!

YES! YES! YES! You *can* get in good husband practice long before your future wife shows up on the scene.

Few things are more attractive to a good woman than a man who is the best brother, son, uncle, cousin (or even father) she has ever seen.

Be a blessing to the women God has placed in your life and put yourself in position to be blessed by the special woman God wants in your life.

And the Lord God said, It is not good that the man should be alone; I will make him an help meet for him.

GENESIS 2:18

Whoso findeth a wife findeth a good thing, and obtaineth favour of the LORD.

PROVERBS 18:22

Blessed is every one that feareth the LORD; that walketh in his ways.

For thou shalt eat the labour of thine hands: happy shalt thou be, and it shall be well with thee.

Thy wife shall be as a fruitful vine by the sides of thine house: thy children like olive plants round about thy table.

Behold, that thus shall the man be blessed that feareth the LORD.

PSALMS 128:1–4

The words of king Lemuel, the prophecy that his mother taught him.

What, my son? and what, the son of my womb? and what, the son of my vows?

Give not thy strength unto women, nor thy ways to that which destroyeth kings.

It is not for kings, O Lemuel, it is not for kings to drink wine; nor for princes strong drink:

Lest they drink, and forget the law, and pervert the judgment of any of the afflicted.

Give strong drink unto him that is ready to perish, and wine unto those that be of heavy hearts.

Let him drink, and forget his poverty, and remember his misery no more.

Open thy mouth for the dumb in the cause of all such as are appointed to destruction.

Open thy mouth, judge righteously, and plead the cause of the poor and needy.

Who can find a virtuous woman? for her price is far above rubies.

The heart of her husband doth safely trust in her, so that he shall have no need of spoil.

She will do him good and not evil all the days of her life.

She seeketh wool, and flax, and worketh willingly with her hands.

She is like the merchant's ships; she bringeth her food from afar.

She riseth also while it is yet night, and giveth meat to her household, and a portion to her maidens.

She considereth a field, and buyeth it: with the fruit of her hands she planteth a vineyard.

She girdeth her loins with strength, and strengtheneth her arms.

She perceiveth that her merchandise is good: her candle goeth not out by night.

She layeth her hands to the spindle, and her hands hold the distaff.

She stretcheth out her hand to the poor; yea, she reacheth forth her hands to the needy.

She is not afraid of the snow for her household: for all her household are clothed with scarlet.

She maketh herself coverings of tapestry; her clothing is silk and purple.

Her husband is known in the gates, when he sitteth among the elders of the land.

She maketh fine linen, and selleth it; and delivereth girdles unto the merchant.

Strength and honour are her clothing; and she shall rejoice in time to come.

She openeth her mouth with wisdom; and her tongue is the law of kindness.

She looketh well to the ways of her household, and eateth not the bread of idleness.

Her children arise up, and call her blessed; her husband also, and he praiseth her.

Many daughters have done virtuously, but thou excellest them all.

Favour is deceitful, and beauty is vain: but a woman that feareth the LORD, she shall be praised.

Give her of the fruit of her hands; and let her own works praise her in the gates.

PROVERBS 31:1–31

*B*e ye not unequally yoked together with unbelievers: for what fellowship hath righteousness with unrighteousness? and what communion hath light with darkness?

And what concord hath Christ with Belial? or what part hath he that believeth with an infidel?

And what agreement hath the temple of God with idols? for ye are the temple of the living God; as God hath said, I will dwell in them, and walk in them; and I will be their God, and they shall be my people.

Wherefore come out from among them, and be ye separate, saith the Lord, and touch not the unclean thing; and I will receive you,

And will be a Father unto you, and ye shall be my sons and daughters, saith the Lord Almighty.

2 CORINTHIANS 6:14–18

*N*evertheless let every one of you in particular so love his wife even as himself; and the wife see that she reverence her husband.

EPHESIANS 5:33

*A*nd this is the confidence that we have in him, that, if we ask any thing according to his will, he heareth us:

And if we know that he hear us, whatsoever we ask,

204 God's Word for the Unmarried Believer

we know that we have the petitions that we desired of him.

1 JOHN 5:14-15

𝓑e careful for nothing; but in every thing by prayer and supplication with thanksgiving let your requests be made known unto God.

And the peace of God, which passeth all understanding, shall keep your hearts and minds through Christ Jesus.

PHILIPPIANS 4:6-7

𝓣herefore shall a man leave his father and his mother, and shall cleave unto his wife: and they shall be one flesh.

And they were both naked, the man and his wife, and were not ashamed.

GENESIS 2:24-25

𝓐nd ye are complete in him, which is the head of all principality and power:

COLOSSIANS 2:10

𝓓elight thyself also in the LORD; and he shall give thee the desires of thine heart.

Commit thy way unto the LORD; trust also in him; and he shall bring it to pass.

PSALMS 37:4-5

Rest in the LORD, and wait patiently for him: fret not thyself because of him who prospereth in his way, because of the man who bringeth wicked devices to pass.

PSALMS 37:7

The integrity of the upright shall guide them: but the perverseness of transgressors shall destroy them.

PROVERBS 11:3

But he that is married careth for the things that are of the world, how he may please his wife.

1 CORINTHIANS 7:33

To every thing there is a season, a time to every purpose under the heaven:

ECCLESIASTES 3:1

He hath made every thing beautiful in his time: also he hath set the world in their heart, so that no man can find out the work that God maketh from the beginning to the end.

ECCLESIASTES 3:11

For with God nothing shall be impossible.

LUKE 1:37

$\mathcal{L}$et us hold fast the profession of our faith without wavering; (for he is faithful that promised;)

HEBREWS 10:23

$\mathcal{B}$ut seek ye first the kingdom of God, and his righteousness; and all these things shall be added unto you.

MATTHEW 6:33

$\mathcal{B}$lessed is every one that feareth the LORD; that walketh in his ways.

For thou shalt eat the labour of thine hands: happy shalt thou be, and it shall be well with thee.

Thy wife shall be as a fruitful vine by the sides of thine house: thy children like olive plants round about thy table.

Behold, that thus shall the man be blessed that feareth the LORD.

The LORD shall bless thee out of Zion: and thou shalt see the good of Jerusalem all the days of thy life.

Yea, thou shalt see thy children's children, and peace upon Israel.

PSALMS 128:1–6

$\mathcal{P}$raise ye the LORD. Blessed is the man that feareth the LORD, that delighteth greatly in his commandments.

His seed shall be mighty upon earth: the generation of the upright shall be blessed.

Wealth and riches shall be in his house: and his righteousness endureth for ever.

Unto the upright there ariseth light in the darkness: he is gracious, and full of compassion, and righteous.

A good man sheweth favour, and lendeth: he will guide his affairs with discretion.

Surely he shall not be moved for ever: the righteous shall be in everlasting remembrance.

He shall not be afraid of evil tidings: his heart is fixed, trusting in the LORD.

His heart is established, he shall not be afraid, until he see his desire upon his enemies.

He hath dispersed, he hath given to the poor; his righteousness endureth for ever; his horn shall be exalted with honour.

The wicked shall see it, and be grieved; he shall gnash with his teeth, and melt away: the desire of the wicked shall perish.

PSALMS 112:1–10

*Y*e are the light of the world. A city that is set on an hill cannot be hid.

MATTHEW 5:14

But I would have you without carefulness. He that is unmarried careth for the things that belong to the Lord, how he may please the Lord:

1 CORINTHIANS 7:32

But I would have you know, that the head of every man is Christ; and the head of the woman is the man; and the head of Christ is God.

1 CORINTHIANS 11:3

And let us not be weary in well doing: for in due season we shall reap, if we faint not.

GALATIANS 6:9

And the LORD shall guide thee continually, and satisfy thy soul in drought, and make fat thy bones: and thou shalt be like a watered garden, and like a spring of water, whose waters fail not.

ISAIAH 58:11

Cast not away your confidence, which hath great recompence of reward.

For ye have need of patience, that, after ye have done the will of God, ye might receive the promise.

HEBREWS 10:35-56

But they that wait upon the LORD shall renew their strength; they shall mount up with wings as eagles; they shall run, and not be weary; and they shall walk, and not faint.

ISAIAH 40:31

Salvation

It's the beginning.

THE FIRST STEP to a life of seeing ourselves the way God does is to get with His program—salvation.

If you have not already done it, open your mouth right now and admit to the Father that you are a sinner. Tell Him that you believe He gave His only son, Jesus, to die for your sins, and that you believe Jesus rose from the dead.

Finished? Congratulations on the beginning of your new life in Christ!

But what saith it? The word is nigh thee, even in thy mouth, and in thy heart: that is, the word of faith, which we preach;

That is thou shalt confess with thy mouth the

Lord Jesus, and shalt believe in thine heart that God hath raised him from the dead, thou shalt be saved.

For with the heart man believeth unto righteousness; and with the mouth confession is made unto salvation.

ROMANS 10:8–10

For whosoever shall call upon the name of the Lord shall be saved.

ROMANS 10:13

For if by one man's offence death reigned by one; much more they which receive abundance of grace and of the gift of righteousness shall reign in life by one, Jesus Christ.)

ROMANS 5:17

Behold, the LORD's hand is not shortened, that it cannot save; neither his ear heavy, that it cannot hear:

ISAIAH 59:1

Wherefore he is able also to save them to the uttermost that come unto God by him, seeing he ever liveth to maketh intercession for them.

HEBREWS 7:25

For by grace are ye saved through faith; and that not of yourselves: it is the gift of God:

Not of works, lest any man should boast.

EPHESIANS 2:8–9

For God so loved the world, that he gave his only begotten Son, that whosoever believeth in him should not perish, but have everlasting life.

For God sent not his Son into the world to condemn the world; but that the world through him might be saved.

JOHN 3:16–17

But as many as received him, to them gave he power to become the sons of God, even to them that believe on his name:

Which were born, not of blood, nor of the will of the flesh, nor of the will of man, but of God.

JOHN 1:12–13

Marvel not at this: for the hour is coming, in the which all that are in the graves shall hear his voice.

JOHN 5:28

All that the Father giveth me shall come unto me; and him that cometh to me I will in no wise cast out.

JOHN 6:37

And they said, Believe on the Lord Jesus Christ, and thou shalt be saved, and thy house.

ACTS 16:31

Jesus answered and said unto him, Verily, verily, I say unto thee, Except a man be born again, he cannot see the kingdom of God.

Nicodemus saith unto him, How can a man be born when he is old? can he enter the second time into his mother's womb, and be born?

Jesus answered, Verily, verily, I say unto thee, Except a man be born of water and of the Spirit, he cannot enter into the kingdom of God.

That which is born of the flesh is flesh; and that which is born of the Spirit is spirit.

Marvel not that I said unto thee, Ye must be born again.

JOHN 3:3-7

Self-Control

Who are you going to let run this show?

WE ARE TOLD in the Bible to work out our own salvation. That means we alone are responsible for glorifying God with our personal actions and words.

When we fall down on our duties, we give the enemy an opportunity to do his thing and tap-dance on our heads.

As someone once said, "Sin will always take you farther than you mean to go and keep you longer than you planned to stay!"

We know the areas of our lives that we need to keep in check. Cover them daily in prayer.

Flee fornication. Every sin that a man doeth is without the body; but he that committeth fornication sinneth against his own body.

What? know ye not that your body is the temple of the Holy Ghost which is in you, which ye have of God, and ye are not your own?

For ye are bought with a price: therefore glorify God in your body, and in your spirit, which are God's.

1 CORINTHIANS 6:18–20

What? Know ye not that he which is joined to an harlot is one body? for two, saith he, shall be one flesh.

But he that is joined unto the Lord is one spirit.

1 CORINTHIANS 6:16–17

Know ye not that your bodies are the members of Christ? shall I then take the members of Christ, and make them the members of an harlot? God forbid.

1 CORINTHIANS 6:15

Love not the world, neither the things that are in the world. If any man love the world, the love of the Father is not in him.

For all that is in the world, the lust of the flesh, and the lust of the eyes, and the pride of life, is not of the Father, but is of the world.

1 JOHN 2:15–16

For with God nothing shall be impossible.

LUKE 1:37

I beseech you therefore, brethren, by the mercies of God, that ye present your bodies a living sacrifice, holy, acceptable unto God, which is your reasonable service.

And be not conformed to this world: but be ye transformed by the renewing of your mind, that ye may prove what is that good, and acceptable, and perfect, will of God.

ROMANS 12:1–2

So then they that are in the flesh cannot please God.

ROMANS 8:8

There is therefore now no condemnation to them which are in Christ Jesus, who walk not after the flesh, but after the Spirit.

For the law of the Spirit of life in Christ Jesus hath made me free from the law of sin and death.

ROMANS 8:1–2

There is a way which seemeth right unto a man, but the end thereof are the ways of death.

PROVERBS 14:12

My son, if sinners entice thee, consent thou not.

PROVERBS 1:10

Enter not into the path of the wicked, and go not in the way of evil men.

Avoid it, pass not by it, turn from it, and pass away.

PROVERBS 4:14–15

Wherefore come out from among them, and be ye separate, saith the Lord, and touch not the unclean thing; and I will receive you.

And will be a Father unto you, and ye shall be my sons and daughters, saith the Lord Almighty.

2 CORINTHIANS 6:17–18

Casting down imaginations, and every high thing that exalted itself against the knowledge of God, and bringing into captivity every thought to the obedience of Christ;

2 CORINTHIANS 10:5

For in that he himself hath suffered being tempted, he is able to succour them that are tempted.

HEBREWS 2:18

Marriage is honourable in all, and the bed undefiled: but whoremongers and adulterers God will judge.

HEBREWS 13:4

I can do all things through Christ which strengtheneth me.

PHILIPPIANS 4:13

Finally, brethren, whatsoever things are true, whatsoever things are honest, whatsoever things are just, whatsoever things are pure, whatsoever things are lovely, whatsoever things are of good report; if there be any virtue, and if there be any praise, think on these things.

PHILIPPIANS 4:8

But the fruit of the Spirit is love, joy, peace, longsuffering, gentleness, goodness, faith,

GALATIANS 5:22

And they that are Christ's have crucified the flesh with the affections and lusts.

If we live in the Spirit, let us also walk in the Spirit.

GALATIANS 5:24-25

This I say then, Walk in the Spirit, and ye shall not fulfil the lust of the flesh.

GALATIANS 5:16

I call heaven and earth to record this day against you, that I have set before you life and death, blessing and cursing: therefore choose life, that both thou and thy seed may live:

DEUTERONOMY 30:19

Our help is in the name LORD, who made the heaven and earth.

PSALMS 124:8

Finally, my brethren, be strong in the Lord, and in the power of his might.

Put on the whole armour of God, that ye may be able to stand against the wiles of the devil.

EPHESIANS 6:10-11

Self-Esteem

*Whom will you believe—the magazines
or the King of Kings?*

IF YOU DON'T KNOW what the Almighty God thinks
about you, then don't you think it's about time you did
something to find out?

Then, if what you think doesn't match up with
what He says, you'd better change what you think!

This is the book of the generations of Adam. In the
day that God created man, in the likeness of God
made he him;

Male and female created he them; and blessed
them, and called their name Adam, in the day when
they were created.

GENESIS 5:1–2

And God said, Let us make man in our image, after our likeness: and let them have dominion over the fish of the sea, and over the fowl of the air, and over the cattle, and over all the earth, and over every creeping thing that creepeth upon the earth.

So God created man in his own image, in the image of God created he him; male and female created he them.

GENESIS 1:26–27

And ye are complete in him, which is the head of all principality and power:

COLOSSIANS 2:10

Know ye not that ye are the temple of God, and that the Spirit of God dwelleth in you?

1 CORINTHIANS 3:16

And ye are Christ's; and Christ is God's.

1 CORINTHIANS 3:23

Cast not away therefore your confidence, which hath great recompence of reward.

HEBREWS 10:35

The LORD hath appeared of old unto me, saying, Yea, I have loved thee with an everlasting love: therefore with lovingkindness have I drawn thee.

JEREMIAH 31:3

In my distress I cried unto the LORD, and he heard me.

PSALMS 120:1

I love them that love me; and those that seek me early shall find me.

PROVERBS 8:17

For with God nothing shall be impossible.

LUKE 1:37

For ye are bought with a price: therefore glorify God in your body, and in your spirit, which are God's.

1 CORINTHIANS 6:20

There is therefore now no condemnation to them which are in Christ Jesus, who walk not after the flesh, but after the Spirit.

ROMANS 8:1

The Spirit itself beareth witness with our spirit, that we are the children of God:

ROMANS 8:16

Temptation

*It's just another situation that has to bow
to the Name of Jesus.*

THERE ARE THOSE DAYS when just about everything (or everyone) we know we should not look at
hard; like or desire is in our face. How do we fight it—
especially when temptation is just there for the taking?

We don't. We let the authority and the Name of
Jesus do our fighting for us. Remember, Jesus was God,
but walked the earth as a man. He knows about temptation—all types—because He faced the same chal-
lenges we do.

Who are you gonna call? Jesus! Give it to Him and
let Him be your Temptation Buster.

Blessed is the man that endureth temptation: for when he is tried, he shall receive the crown of life, which the Lord hath promised to them that love him.

JAMES 1:12

There is a way that seemeth right unto a man, but the end thereof are the ways of death.

PROVERBS 14:12

But whoso hearkeneth unto me shall dwell safely, and shall be quiet from fear of evil.

PROVERBS 1:33

The LORD is good, a strong hold in the day of trouble; and he knoweth them that trust in him.

NAHUM 1:7

I can do all things through Christ which strengtheneth me.

PHILIPPIANS 4:13

Be ye not unequally yoked together with unbelievers: for what fellowship hath righteousness with unrighteousness? and what communion hath light with darkness?

And what concord hath Christ with Belial? or what part hath he that believeth with an infidel?

And what agreement hath the temple of God with idols? for ye are the temple of the living God; as God hath said, I will dwell in them, and walk in them; and I will be their God, and they shall be my people.

Wherefore come out from among them, and be ye separate, saith the Lord, and touch not the unclean thing; and I will receive you.

And will be a Father unto you, and ye shall be my sons and daughters, saith the Lord Almighty.

2 CORINTHIANS 6:14-18

Be ye strong therefore, and let not your hands be weak: for your work shall be rewarded.

2 CHRONICLES 15:7

Now know I that the LORD saveth his anointed; he will hear him from his holy heaven with the saving strength of his right hand.

PSALMS 20:6

For he shall deliver the needy when he crieth; the poor also, and him that hath no helper.

PSALMS 72:12

Know ye not that ye are the temple of God, and that the Spirit of God dwelleth in you?

1 CORINTHIANS 3:16

Therefore, my beloved brethren, be ye stedfast, unmoveable, always abounding in the work of the Lord, forasmuch as ye know that your labour is not in vain in the Lord.

1 CORINTHIANS 15:58

The eternal God is thy refuge, and underneath are the everlasting arms: and he shall thrust out the enemy from before thee; and shall say, Destroy them.

DEUTERONOMY 33:27

Come unto me, all ye that labour and are heavy laden, and I will give you rest.

Take my yoke upon you, and learn of me; for I am meek and lowly in heart: and ye shall find rest unto your souls.

For my yoke is easy, and my burden is light.

MATTHEW 11:28–30

For in that he himself hath suffered being tempted, he is able to succour them that are tempted.

HEBREWS 2:18

Since thou wast precious in my sight, thou has been honourable, and I have loved thee: therefore will I give men for thee, and people for thy life.

ISAIAH 43:4

No weapon that is formed against thee shall prosper; and every tongue that shall rise against thee in judgment thou shalt condemn. This is the heritage of the servants of the LORD, and their righteousness is of me, saith the LORD.

ISAIAH 54:17

Now unto him that is able to do exceeding abundantly above all that we ask or think, according to the power that worketh in us,

EPHESIANS 3:20

He shall cover thee with his feathers, and under his wings shalt thou trust: his truth shall be thy shield and buckler.

Thou shalt not be afraid for the terror by night; nor for the arrow that flieth by day;

Nor for the pestilence that walketh in darkness; nor for the destruction that wasteth at noonday.

A thousand shall fall at thy side, and ten thousand at thy right hand; but it shall not come nigh thee.

PSALMS 91:4–7

When a man's ways please the LORD, he maketh even his enemies to be at peace with him.

PROVERBS 16:7

Trust in the LORD with all thine heart; and lean not unto thine own understanding.

In all thy ways acknowledge him, and he shall direct thy paths.

PROVERBS 3:5–6

And they that are Christ's have crucified the flesh with the affections and lusts.

If we live in the Spirit, let us also walk in the Spirit.

GALATIANS 5:24–25

Submit yourselves therefore to God. Resist the devil, and he will flee from you.

JAMES 4:7

Blessed is the man that trusteth in the LORD, and whose hope the LORD is.

For he shall be as a tree planted by the waters, and that spreadeth out her roots by the river, and shall not see when heat cometh, but her leaf shall be green; and shall not be careful in the year of drought, neither shall cease from yielding fruit.

JEREMIAH 17:7–8

Be ye not unequally yoked together with unbelievers: for what fellowship hath righteousness with unrighteousness? and what communion hath light with darkness?

And what concord hath Christ with Belial? or what part hath he that believeth with an infidel?

And what agreement hath the temple of God with idols? for ye are the temple of the living God; as God hath said, I will dwell in them, and walk in them; and I will be their God, and they shall be my people.

Wherefore come out from among them, and be ye separate, saith the Lord, and touch not the unclean thing; and I will receive you,

And will be a Father unto you, and ye shall be my sons and daughters, saith the Lord Almighty.

2 CORINTHIANS 6:14–18

*T*here is therefore now no condemnation to them which are in Christ Jesus, who walk not after the flesh, but after the Spirit.

For the law of the Spirit of life in Christ Jesus hath made me free from the law of sin and death.

ROMANS 8:1–2

I beseech you therefore, brethren, by the mercies of God, that ye present your bodies a living sacrifice, holy, acceptable unto God, which is your reasonable service.

And be not conformed to this world: but be ye transformed by the renewing of your mind, that ye may prove what is that good, and acceptable, and perfect, will of God.

ROMANS 12:1-2

Too Old? For What?

God is strength and fire shut up in your bones.

WHEN WE WORRY that we are too old to get married or to start a new business or to dream new visions, we are only meditating on a lie of the devil. This is your season!

You can do all things because He strengthens you. The long years of your life are a blessing from God. Celebrate them!

My flesh and my heart faileth: but God is the strength of my heart, and my portion for ever.

PSALMS 73:26

The righteous shall flourish like the palm tree: he shall grow like a cedar in Lebanon.

Those that be planted in the house of the LORD shall flourish in the courts of our God.

They shall still bring forth fruit in old age; they shall be fat and flourishing;

PSALMS 92:12–14

Bless the LORD, O my soul, and forget not all his benefits:

Who forgiveth all thine iniquities; who healeth all thy diseases;

Who redeemeth thy life from destruction; who crowneth thee with lovingkindness and tender mercies;

Who satisfieth thy mouth with good things; so that thy youth is renewed like the eagle's.

PSALMS 103:2–5

Be of good courage, and he shall strengthen your heart, all ye that hope in the LORD.

PSALMS 31:24

I know both how to be abased, and I know how to abound: every where and in all things I am instructed both to be full and to be hungry, both to abound and to suffer need.

I can do all things through Christ which strengtheneth me.

PHILIPPIANS 4:12–13

That the aged men be sober, grave, temperate, sound in faith, in charity, in patience.

The aged women likewise, that they be in behaviour as becometh holiness, not false accusers, not given to much wine, teachers of good things;

That they may teach the young women to be sober, to love their husbands, to love their children,

To be discreet, chaste, keepers at home, good, obedient to their own husbands, that the word of God be not blasphemed.

Titus 2:2–5

For verily I say unto you, That whosoever shall say unto this mountain, Be thou removed, and be thou cast into the sea; and shall not doubt in his heart, but shall believe that those things which he saith shall come to pass; he shall have whatsoever he saith.

Mark 11:23

But blessed are your eyes, for they see: and your ears, for they hear.

Matthew 13:16

For with God nothing shall be impossible.

Luke 1:37

For which cause we faint not; but though our outward man perish, yet the inward man is renewed day by day.

2 CORINTHIANS 4:16

The days of our years are threescore years and ten; and if by reason of strength they be fourscore years, yet is their strength labour and sorrow; for it is soon cut off, and we fly away.

PSALMS 90:10

For by me thy days shall be multiplied, and the years of thy life shall be increased.

PROVERBS 9:11

The fear of the LORD prolongeth days: but the years of the wicked shall be shortened.

PROVERBS 10:27

Fear thou not; for I am with thee: be not dismayed; for I am thy God: I will strengthen thee; yea, I will help thee; yea, I will uphold thee with the right hand of my righteousness.

ISAIAH 41:10

And even to your old age I am he; and even to hoar hairs will I carry you: I have made, and I will bear; even I will carry, and will deliver you.

ISAIAH 46:4

Be ye strong therefore, and let not your hands be weak; for your work shall be rewarded.

2 CHRONICLES 15:7

What shall we then say to these things? If God be for us, who can be against us?

ROMANS 8:31

Unmarried and Loving It

God and I are having a great time!

SOMETIMES IT SEEMS as if unmarrieds go through their lives almost as if they are asleep, just waiting to get married to finally wake up and begin to live.

That's not how it is supposed to be.

The time of our lives we live without the blessings of a husband or a wife is time to be cherished. And time to be busy.

There is much to be done for the Kingdom of God, and He expects us, as unmarrieds who do not yet have the responsibilities of a mate, to do it.

Fill your life with the work and the joy of the Lord and He will fill you with an unspeakable good time. Wake up. Joy is here!

*B*ut I would have you without carefulness. He that is unmarried careth for the things that belong to the Lord, how he may please Lord:

1 Corinthians 7:32

*B*ut ye are a chosen generation, a royal priesthood, an holy nation, a peculiar people; that ye should shew forth the praises of him who hath called you out of darkness into his marvellous light:

1 Peter 2:9

*W*hatsoever thy hand findeth to do, do it with thy might; for there is no work, nor device, nor knowledge, nor wisdom, in the grave, whither thou goest.

Ecclesiastes 9:10

*N*ot that I speak in respect of want: for I have learned, in whatsoever state I am, therewith to be content.

I know both how to be abased, and I know how to abound: every where and in all things I am instructed both to be full and to be hungry, both to abound and to suffer need.

I can do all things through Christ which strengtheneth me.

Philippians 4:11–13

𝒷ut let all those that put their trust in thee rejoice: let them ever shout for joy, because thou defendest them: let them also that love thy name be joyful in thee.

For thou, LORD, wilt bless the righteous; with favour wilt thou compass him as with a shield.

PSALMS 5:11–12

𝒯he steps of a good man are ordered by the LORD: and he delighteth in his way.

PSALMS 37:23

ℐf ye then be risen with Christ, seek those things which are above, where Christ sitteth on the right hand of God.

Set your affection on things above, not on things on the earth.

COLOSSIANS 3:1–2

𝒯hat ye might walk worthy of the Lord unto all pleasing, being fruitful in every good work, and increasing in the knowledge of God;

COLOSSIANS 1:10

𝒜nd we have known and believed the love that God hath to us. God is love; and he that dwelleth in love dwelleth in God, and God in him.

1 JOHN 4:16

But seek ye first the kingdom of God, and his righteousness; and all these things shall be added unto you.

Take therefore no thought for the morrow: for the morrow shall take thought for the things of itself. Sufficient unto the day is the evil thereof.

MATTHEW 6:33–34

Unmarried and a Parent

God invented Mommies and Daddies,
and He can meet the need.

WHILE *LOVING CHILDREN* may be a joy, *raising* them is no joke, especially if you are unmarried. Sure, you may have good friends and dedicated family, but still you worry that no one can take the place of that mother or father who is not around.

But God can. And raising your children to know the love of God is the first step to plugging that empty place in their heart that can be left by the absence of a parent.

If we will let Him, God will be whatever we need for ourselves and for our children.

The LORD is good, a strong hold in the day of trouble; and he knoweth them that trust in him.

NAHUM 1:7

And Jesus increased in wisdom and stature, and in favour with God and man.

LUKE 2:52

But if any provide not for his own, and specially for those of his own house, he hath denied the faith, and is worse than an infidel.

1 TIMOTHY 5:8

One that ruleth well his own house, having his children in subjection with all gravity;

(For if a man know not how to rule his own house, how shall he take care of the church of God?)

1 TIMOTHY 3:4–5

And these words, which I command thee this day, shall be in thine heart:

And thou shalt teach them diligently unto thy children, and shalt talk of them when thou sittest in thine house, and when thou walkest by the way, and when thou liest down, and when thou risest up.

And thou shalt bind them for a sign upon thine hand, and they shall be as frontlets between thine eyes.

And thou shalt write them upon the posts of thy house, and on thy gates.

DEUTERONOMY 6:6-9

$\mathcal{I}$ call heaven and earth to record this day against you, that I have set before you life and death, blessing and cursing: therefore choose life, that both thou and thy seed may live:

That thou mayest love the LORD thy God, and that thou mayest obey his voice, and that thou mayest cleave unto him: for he is thy life, and the length of thy days: that thou mayest dwell in the land which the LORD sware unto thy fathers, to Abraham, to Isaac, and to Jacob, to give them.

DEUTERONOMY 30:19-20

$\mathcal{A}$nd the LORD shall make thee the head, and not the tail; and thou shalt be above only, and thou shalt not be beneath; if that thou hearken unto the commandments of the LORD thy God, which I command thee this day, to observe and to do them:

DEUTERONOMY 28:13

$\mathcal{A}$nd he took a child, and set him in the midst of them: and when he had taken him in his arms, he said unto them,

Whosoever shall receive one of such children in

my name, receiveth me: and whosoever shall receive me, receiveth not me, but him that sent me.

MARK 9:36-37

*N*ow therefore go, and I will be with thy mouth, and teach thee what thou shalt say.

EXODUS 4:12

*B*ut whoso shall offend one of these little ones which believe in me, it were better for him that a millstone were hanged about his neck, and that he were drowned in the depth of the sea.

MATTHEW 18:6

*T*ake heed that ye despise not one of these little ones; for I say unto you, That in heaven their angels do always behold the face of my Father which is in heaven.

MATTHEW 18:10

*E*ven so it is not the will of your Father which is in heaven, that one of these little ones should perish.

MATTHEW 18:14

*B*ut blessed are your eyes, for they see: and your ears, for they hear.

MATTHEW 13:16

What shall we then say to these things? If God be for us, who can be against us?

ROMANS 8:31

Fathers, provoke not your children to anger, lest they be discouraged.

COLOSSIANS 3:21

But my God shall supply all your need according to his riches in glory by Christ Jesus.

PHILIPPIANS 4:19

And all thy children shall be taught of the LORD; and great shall be the peace of thy children.

ISAIAH 54:13

Fear thou not; for I am with thee: be not dismayed; for I am thy God: I will strengthen thee; yea, I will help thee; yea, I will uphold thee with the right hand of my righteousness.

ISAIAH 41:10

But thus saith the LORD, Even the captives of the mighty shall be taken away, and the prey of the terrible shall be delivered: for I will contend with him that contendeth with thee, and I will save thy children.

ISAIAH 49:25

The just man walketh in his integrity: his children are blessed after him.

PROVERBS 20:7

Through wisdom is an house builded; and by understanding it is established:

PROVERBS 24:3

Trust in the LORD with all thine heart; and lean not unto thine own understanding.

PROVERBS 3:5

Open rebuke is better than secret love.

PROVERBS 27:5

Train up a child in the way he should go: and when he is old, he will not depart from it.

PROVERBS 22:6

Foolishness is bound in the heart of a child; but the rod of correction shall drive it far from him.

PROVERBS 22:15

The father of the righteous shall greatly rejoice: and he that begetteth a wise child shall have joy of him.

PROVERBS 23:24

$\mathcal{F}$or the LORD giveth wisdom: out of his mouth cometh knowledge and understanding.

He layeth up sound wisdom for the righteous: he is a buckler to them that walk uprightly.

PROVERBS 2:6-7

$\mathcal{C}$orrect thy son, and he shall give thee rest; yea, he shall give delight unto thy soul.

PROVERBS 29:17

$\mathcal{A}$ good man leaveth an inheritance to his children's children: and the wealth of the sinner is laid up for the just.

PROVERBS 13:22

$\mathcal{I}$n the fear of the LORD is strong confidence: and his children shall have a place of refuge.

PROVERBS 14:26

$\mathcal{L}$o, children are an heritage of the LORD: and the fruit of the womb is his reward.

PSALMS 127:3

$\mathcal{I}$ will bless the LORD, who hath given me counsel: my reins also instruct me in the night seasons.

PSALMS 16:7

I have set the LORD always before me: because he is at my right hand, I shall not be moved.

Therefore my heart is glad, and my glory rejoiceth: my flesh also shall rest in hope.

PSALMS 16:8–9

*F*or thou art my rock and my fortress; therefore for thy name's sake lead me, and guide me.

PSALMS 31:3

I will instruct thee and teach thee in the way which thou shalt go: I will guide thee with mine eye.

PSALMS 32:8

When Even Your Troubles Have Trouble

God is still on the throne.

THERE ARE TIMES when we all feel as though if one more thing goes wrong or if one more responsibility gets piled on us, we will explode!

Don't blow *up*, blow *out*. That's right, take a big breath and exhale.

Then take a moment to remember that the God who brought the Hebrew slaves out of Israel is still on the throne. Remember that the God who gave that little boy David the nerve to run *toward* his Goliath instead of in the other direction is still on the throne, and most of all remember that the same God who pulled your fat out of the fire a million times before is still on the throne.

Then go on with your day and your life, always expecting the God you serve to make His move on your behalf!

*A*nd call upon me in the day of trouble: I will deliver thee, and thou shalt glorify me.

PSALMS 50:15

Many are the afflictions of the righteous: but the LORD delivereth him out of them all.

PSALMS 34:19

*T*hey shall bear thee up in their hands, lest thou dash thy foot against a stone.

Thou shalt tread upon the lion and adder: the young lion and the dragon shalt thou trample under feet.

Because he hath set his love upon me, therefore will I deliver him: I will set him on high, because he hath known my name.

He shall call upon me, and I will answer him: I will be with him in trouble; I will deliver him, and honour him.

With long life will I satisfy him, and shew him my salvation.

PSALMS 91:12–16

Therefore I say unto you, Take no thought for your life, what ye shall eat, or what ye shall drink; nor yet for your body, what ye shall put on. Is not the life more than meat, and the body than raiment?

Behold the fowls of the air: for they sow not, neither do they reap, nor gather into barns; yet your heavenly Father feedeth them. Are ye not much better than they?

Which of you by taking thought can add one cubit unto his stature?

MATTHEW 6:25–27

And he said, My presence shall go with thee, and I will give thee rest.

EXODUS 33:14

If ye then, being evil, know how to give good gifts unto your children: how much more shall your heavenly Father give the Holy Spirit to them that ask him?

LUKE 11:13

There remaineth therefore a rest to the people of God.

For he that is entered into his rest, he also hath ceased from his own works, as God did from his.

Let us labour therefore to enter into that rest, lest any man fall after the same example of unbelief.

HEBREWS 4:9–11

The LORD is my shepherd; I shall not want.

He maketh me to lie down in green pastures: he leadeth me beside the still waters.

He restoreth my soul: he leadeth me in the paths of righteousness for his name's sake.

Yea, though I walk through the valley of the shadow of death, I will fear no evil: for thou art with me; thy rod and thy staff they comfort me.

PSALMS 23:1–4

In my distress I called upon the LORD, and cried unto my God: he heard my voice out of his temple, and my cry came before him, even into his ears.

PSALMS 18:6

My brethren, count it all joy when ye fall into divers temptations;

Knowing this, that the trying of your faith worketh patience.

JAMES 1:2–3

We are trouble on every side, yet not distressed; we are perplexed, but not in despair;

Persecuted, but not forsaken; cast down, but not destroyed;

2 CORINTHIANS 4:8–9

There hath no temptation taken you but such as is common to man: but God is faithful, who will not suffer you to be tempted above that ye are able; but will with the temptation also make a way to escape, that ye may be able to bear it.

1 CORINTHIANS 10:13

Behold, the eye of the LORD is upon them that fear him, upon them that hope in his mercy;

To deliver their soul from death, and to keep them alive in famine.

Our soul waiteth for the LORD: he is our help and our shield.

For our heart shall rejoice in him, because we have trusted in his holy name.

PSALMS 33:18:21

Why art thou cast down, O my soul? and why art thou disquieted within me? hope thou in God: for I shall yet praise him, who is the health of my countenance, and my God.

PSALMS 42:11

They that sow in tears shall reap in joy.

He that goeth forth and weepeth, bearing precious seed, shall doubtless come again with rejoicing, bringing his sheaves with him.

PSALMS 126:5-6

The righteous cry, and the LORD heareth, and delivereth them out of all their troubles.

PSALMS 34:17

Come unto me, all ye that labour and are heavy laden, and I will give you rest.

Take my yoke upon you, and learn of me; for I am meek and lowly in heart: and ye shall find rest unto your souls.

For my yoke is easy, and my burden is light.

MATTHEW 11:28–30

Behold, I give unto you power to tread on serpents and scorpions, and over all the power of the enemy: and nothing shall by any means hurt you.

LUKE 10:19

Let not your heart be troubled: ye believe in God, believe also in me.

JOHN 14:1

I will not leave you comfortless: I will come to you.

JOHN 14:18

I call heaven and earth to record this day against you, that I have set before you life and death, blessing and cursing: therefore choose life, that both thou and thy seed may live:

DEUTERONOMY 30:19

So that we may boldly say, The Lord is my helper, and I will not fear what man shall do unto me.

HEBREWS 13:6

The eyes of the LORD are upon the righteous, and his ears are open unto their cry.

PSALMS 34:15

The steps of a good man are ordered by the LORD: and he delighteth in his way.

Though he fall, he shall not be utterly cast down: for the LORD upholdeth him with his hand.

PSALMS 37:23–24

The name of the LORD is a strong tower: the righteous runneth into it, and is safe.

PROVERBS 18:10

For his anger endureth but a moment; in his favour is life: weeping may endure for a night, but joy cometh in the morning.

PSALMS 30:5

Work That Body

How are you treating His Temple?

OUR BODIES are *so* stupid.

They tell us that they don't like exercise. Then, when we force it on them for about a week, they begin to crave it and tell us that they want it.

That's why we can't give our bodies the stuff they *think* they want. God has told us that our bodies belong to Him. How many of us can say that if He asked for our body back today, He would be happy with what He got?

Let's stop allowing our bodies to tell us they are sleepy when it is time to exercise; and that they want junk food when it is time for a nutritious meal.

Let's take care of what God has given us just as we would any other precious gift.

❈

*B*eloved, I wish above all things that thou mayest prosper and be in health, even as thy soul prospereth.

3 JOHN 2

*L*et your moderation be known unto all men. The Lord is at hand.

PHILIPPIANS 4:5

I call heaven and earth to record this day against you, that I have set before you life and death, blessing and cursing: therefore choose life, that both thou and thy seed may live:

DEUTERONOMY 30:19

Know ye not that ye are the temple of God, and that the Spirit of God dwelleth in you?

If any man defile the temple of God, him shall God destroy; for the temple of God is holy, which temple ye are. . . .

And ye are Christ's; and Christ is God's.

1 CORINTHIANS 3:16–17, 23

*B*ut I keep under my body, and bring it into subjection: lest that by any means, when I have preached to others, I myself should be a castaway.

1 CORINTHIANS 9:27

Flee fornication. Every sin that a man doeth is without the body; but he that committeth fornication sinneth against his own body.

What? know ye not that your body is the temple of the Holy Ghost which is in you, which ye have of God, and ye are not your own?

For ye are bought with a price: therefore glorify God in your body, and in your spirit, which are God's.

1 Corinthians 6:18–20

I will instruct thee and teach thee in the way which thou shalt go: I will guide thee with mine eye.

Psalms 32:8

When thou sittest to eat with a ruler, consider diligently what is before thee:

And put a knife to thy throat, if thou be a man given to appetite.

Be not desirous of his dainties: for they are deceitful meat.

Proverbs 23:1–3

Hear thou, my son, and be wise, and guide thine heart in the way.

Be not among winebibbers; among riotous eaters of flesh:

For the drunkard and the glutton shall come to poverty: and drowsiness shall clothe a man with rags.

PROVERBS 23:19–21

J beseech you therefore, brethren, by the mercies of God, that ye present your bodies a living sacrifice, holy, acceptable unto God, which is your reasonable service.

ROMANS 12:1

*B*ut put ye on the Lord Jesus Christ, and make not provision for the flesh, to fulfil the lusts thereof.

ROMANS 13:14

Wisdom

He is the only truth you'll ever need!

IMAGINE ONE of God's children asking Him what should be done in a particular situation.

Then God listens to the problem, takes a deep breath, rubs His chin, scratches His head, sits back down on the Throne, and in a rumbling voice says, "It depends."

Not.

God is not wishy-washy and neither is His Word. Unlike our human wisdom, His wisdom does not depend on the circumstances surrounding a situation but on His love, mercy, and goodness.

The wisdom of God is a precious, holy gift that is available to those of us who diligently seek Him and His Word.

Wisdom is the principal thing; therefore get wisdom: and with all thy getting get understanding.

Exalt her, and she shall promote thee: she shall bring thee to honour, when thou dost embrace her.

PROVERBS 4:7-8

Teach me to do thy will; for thou art my God: thy spirit is good; lead me into the land of uprightness.

PSALMS 143:10

So teach us to number our days, that we may apply our hearts unto wisdom.

PSALMS 90:12

I am thy servant; give me understanding, that I may know thy testimonies.

PSALMS 119:125

The entrance of thy words giveth light; it giveth understanding unto the simple.

PSALMS 119:130

Let my cry come near before thee, O LORD: give me understanding according to thy word.

PSALMS 119:169

*W*hen wisdom entereth into thine heart, and knowledge is pleasant unto thy soul;

Discretion shall preserve thee, understanding shall keep thee:

PROVERBS 2:10-11

*T*o receive the instruction of wisdom, justice, and judgment, and equity;

PROVERBS 1:3

A wise man will hear, and will increase learning; and a man of understanding shall attain unto wise counsels:

PROVERBS 1:15

*T*rust in the LORD with all thine heart; and lean not unto thine own understanding.

In all thy ways acknowledge him, and he shall direct thy paths.

PROVERBS 3:5-6

I wisdom dwell with prudence, and find out knowledge of witty inventions.

PROVERBS 8:12

*C*ounsel is mine, and sound wisdom: I am understanding; I have strength.

PROVERBS 8:14

For wisdom is better than rubies; and all the things that may be desired are not to be compared to it.

PROVERBS 8:11

Through wisdom is an house builded; and by understanding it is established:

And by knowledge shall the chambers be filled with all precious and pleasant riches.

PROVERBS 24:3–4

For the LORD giveth wisdom: out of his mouth cometh knowledge and understanding.

He layeth up sound wisdom for the righteous: he is a buckler to them that walk uprightly.

PROVERBS 2:6–7

Let the word of Christ dwell in you richly in all wisdom; teaching and admonishing one another in psalms and hymns and spiritual songs, singing with grace in your hearts to the Lord.

COLOSSIANS 3:16

For this cause we also, since the day we heard it, do not cease to pray for you, and to desire that ye might be filled with the knowledge of his will in all wisdom and spiritual understanding;

That ye might walk worthy of the Lord unto all

pleasing, being fruitful in every good work, and increasing in the knowledge of God;

Strengthened with all might, according to his glorious power, unto all patience and longsuffering with joyfulness;

COLOSSIANS 1:9–11

*L*et this mind be in you, which was also in Christ Jesus:

PHILIPPIANS 2:5

*I*f any of you lack wisdom, let him ask of God, that giveth to all men liberally, and upbraideth not; and it shall be given him.

But let him ask in faith, nothing wavering. For he that wavereth is like a wave of the sea driven with the wind and tossed.

For let not that man think that he shall receive any thing of the Lord.

JAMES 1:5–7

*B*ut the wisdom that is from above is first pure, then peaceable, gentle, and easy to be intreated, full of mercy and good fruits, without partiality, and without hypocrisy.

JAMES 3:17

But there is a spirit in man: and the inspiration of the Almighty giveth them understanding.

JOB 32:8

For wisdom is a defence, and money is a defence: but the excellency of knowledge is, that wisdom giveth life to them that have it.

ECCLESIASTES 7:12

And he shall set up an ensign for the nations, and shall assemble the outcasts of Israel, and gather together the dispersed of Judah from the four corners of the earth.

ISAIAH 11:12

And wisdom and knowledge shall be the stability of thy times, and strength of salvation: the fear of the LORD is his treasure.

ISAIAH 33:6

Howbeit when he, the Spirit of truth, is come, he will guide you into all truth: for he shall not speak of himself; but whatsoever he shall hear, that shall he speak: and he will shew you things to come.

JOHN 16:13

And I say unto you, Ask, and it shall be given you; seek, and ye shall find; knock, and it shall be opened unto you.

For every one that asketh receiveth; and he that seeketh findeth; and to him that knocketh it shall be opened.

LUKE 11:9–10

Ask, and it shall be given you; seek, and ye shall find; knock, and it shall be opened unto you:

MATTHEW 7:7

I will instruct thee and teach thee in the way which thou shalt go: I will guide thee with mine eye.

PSALMS 32:8

So teach us to number our days, that we may apply our hearts unto wisdom.

PSALMS 90:12

Teach me thy way, O LORD, and lead me in a plain path, because of mine enemies.

PSALMS 27:11

So shall the knowledge of wisdom be unto thy soul: when thou hast found it, then there shall be a reward, and thy expectation shall not be cut off.

PROVERBS 24:14

𝓐 wise man is strong; yea, a man of knowledge increaseth strength.

PROVERBS 24:5

𝓗e that walketh with wise men shall be wise: but a companion of fools shall be destroyed.

PROVERBS 13:20